Sarah Beth Childers is from Huntington, West Virginia, and she lives and writes in Richmond, Indiana, where she is a writer in residence at Earlham College. Previously, she served as a lecturer at West Virginia University and as a visiting professor of creative nonfiction in the low-residency MFA program at West Virginia Wesleyan College. She received her MFA in creative writing from West Virginia University, and she was a recipient of the Olive B. O'Connor Fellowship at Colgate University in 2009. She enjoys reading Victorian novels, playing Chopin nocturnes, quilting, canoeing, and spending time with her Boston terrier and her cat.

Shake Terribly the Earth

Ohio University Press
Series in Race, Ethnicity, and Gender in Appalachia

SERIES EDITORS: MARIE TEDESCO AND CHRIS GREEN

Memphis Tennessee Garrison:
The Remarkable Story of a Black Appalachian Woman,
edited by Ancella R. Bickley and Lynda Ann Ewen

The Tangled Roots of Feminism, Environmentalism,
and Appalachian Literature,
by Elizabeth S. D. Engelhardt

Red, White, Black, and Blue:
A Dual Memoir of Race and Class in Appalachia,
by William R. Drennen Jr. and Kojo (William T.) Jones Jr.,
edited by Dolores M. Johnson

Beyond Hill and Hollow:
Original Readings in Appalachian Women's Studies,
edited by Elizabeth S. D. Engelhardt

Loving Mountains, Loving Men,
by Jeff Mann

Power in the Blood: A Family Narrative,
by Linda Tate

Out of the Mountains: Appalachian Stories,
by Meredith Sue Willis

Negotiating a Perilous Empowerment: Appalachian Women's Literacies,
by Erica Abrams Locklear

Standing Our Ground:
Women, Environmental Justice, and the Fight to End Mountaintop Removal,
by Joyce M. Barry

Shake Terribly the Earth: Stories from an Appalachian Family,
by Sarah Beth Childers

STORIES FROM AN APPALACHIAN FAMILY

SARAH BETH CHILDERS

OHIO UNIVERSITY PRESS + ATHENS

Ohio University Press, Athens, Ohio 45701
ohioswallow.com
© 2013 by Ohio University Press
All rights reserved

Printed in the United States of America
Ohio University Press books are printed on acid-free paper ∞ ™

23 22 21 20 19 18 17 16 15 14 13   5 4 3 2 1

Library of Congress Cataloging-in-Publication Data
Childers, Sarah Beth, [date]
[Essays. Selections]
Shake terribly the earth : stories from an Appalachian family / Sarah Beth Childers.
    pages cm — (Race, ethnicity, and gender in Appalachia)
Summary: "In this linked collection of essays, Sarah Beth Childers takes the stories
she grew up listening to and uses them to make sense of her own personal journey in a
thoughtful, humorous voice born of Appalachian storytelling. Based on interviews, letters,
archives, and memory, these essays bring to life events that touched the entire region:
large families that squeezed into tiny apartments during the Great Depression, a girl who
stepped into a rowboat from a second-story window during Huntington, West Virginia's
1937 flood, brothers who were whisked away to World War II and Vietnam, and a young
man who returned home from the South Pacific and worked his life away as a railroad
engineer. The book also demonstrates the ways our hearts and lives take root in our own
particular patches of Appalachia. The author's mother, Marcy, listens to fundamentalist
Christian radio evangelists, pays for her mentally ill mother's food and cigarettes with a
part-time job at a department store, longs for love, and dreams of becoming a majorette.
Years later, Sarah Beth attends Marcy's chosen church, a Pentecostal congregation where
members blow whistles and run circles around the sanctuary with lampshades on their
heads, and she faces her own love problems at a fundamentalist Baptist school, where she
feels isolated as one of the school's few Pentecostals. Sarah Beth's experiences allow her to
tackle fundamentalist Christianity as an insider, admitting its flaws but also showing the
positive side of such ardent belief. Throughout this book, Sarah Beth seeks to find her own
place within the fundamentalist Christian community and her family, and she looks for the
joy and clarity that often emerge after times of tragedy and change, when the earth shakes
terribly beneath us"— Provided by publisher.
    ISBN 978-0-8214-2061-4 (hardback) — ISBN 978-0-8214-2062-1 (pb) — ISBN 978-0-
8214-4468-9 (electronic)
    1. Childers, Sarah Beth, [date]- 2. Childers, Sarah Beth, [date]——Family. 3. Authors,
American—20th century—Biography. 4. Appalachians (People)—Social life and
customs. 5. Appalachian Region—Religious life and customs. 6. Appalachian Region—
Social conditions. I. Title. II. Title: Stories from an Appalachian family.
PS3603.H554Z46 2013
814'.6—dc23
                                    2013026978

And they shall go into the holes of the rocks, and into the caves of the earth, for fear of the LORD, and for the glory of His majesty, when He ariseth to shake terribly the earth.

In that day a man shall cast his idols of silver, and his idols of gold, which they made each one for himself to worship, to the moles and to the bats;

To go into the clefts of the rocks, and into the tops of the ragged rocks, for fear of the LORD, and for the glory of His majesty, when He ariseth to shake terribly the earth.

Isaiah 2:19–21

For PaPa, Granny, and Mark

Acknowledgments

I am grateful to Jane Pinchin, Jennifer Brice, Patrick O'Keeffe, Peter Balakian, and Colgate University for the Olive B. O'Connor Fellowship and a warm writing community during my year in Hamilton. The fellowship gave me the time and confidence to reimagine my manuscript as a book. Thank you especially to Jennifer, who let me borrow her house, cats, and rabbit.

Thank you to Kevin Oderman, whose generous close reading and belief in my work enabled me to begin and finish this book. Thank you also to his sweet dogs, Figgy and Fay.

Thank you to my sister Rebecca, who tirelessly read every draft of every essay, giving me honest feedback and encouraging me to keep going.

Thank you to Gillian Berchowitz and the readers and editors at Ohio University Press for their help and guidance.

Thank you to my inspiring writing professors at West Virginia University and Marshall University, including Mark Brazaitis, Gail Adams, Ethel Morgan Smith, Ellesa High, Laura Brady, John Van Kirk, Mary Moore, and my dear friend Kateryna Schray. I hear their voices as I write.

Thank you to Jericho Williams for cheering me on through good and bad writing days and for taking me to pick blackberries, feed the cows, and visit his Mawmaw Bean. Thank you to Christina Tremill, Hannah Saltmarsh, Charity Gingerich, Rachel Wilkinson, and Jim Greene for encouragement and support. Thank you also to Sarah Einstein, Ann Claycomb, Lori D'Angelo, Ashley Jenkins, Emily Watson, Kate Klein, and other friends from WVU and Colgate. Their thoughtful comments helped shape these essays.

Thank you to my cat, Arwen, for sitting on the back of my chair while I wrote nearly every page of this book, and my sisters' cats, Joseph and Lizzie, for reminding me to take breaks.

Thank you most of all to my family, for telling me their stories and keeping generations of our family alive through memory. Thank you to my mother, who taught me to read and gave me her writing genes. She inspires me every day with her strength and faith. Thank you to my daddy for his support of my writing, and for teaching me to love Beech Fork and the floodwall. Thank you to Grandpa, who made me feel like a serious writer even when I was twelve years old, writing poems and newspaper articles about my dolls. Thank you to MaMa for telling stories about her sisters and letting my sisters and me play in her closets. Thank you and RTP to my Uncle Bill, for his joy in nature and good writing. Thank you to Aunt Lita and Aunt Anita, who brought their and PaPa's childhood and youth to life for me with their gifted storytelling and humor. Thank you to my siblings, Jennifer, Rebecca, and Joshua, for our shared life and laughter. Thank you for making paper dolls, writing stories about kings and bears, and wearing the shirts I embroidered for you.

The following essays previously appeared in literary journals: "Garbage-Bag Charity" in *SNReview*, "Boat Stories: Three Generations" in *The Tusculum Review*, "Shorn" in *Wigleaf*, and "Ghost Siblings" in *Beside the Point*.

Contents

O Glorious Love   1

Shorn   10

Through a Train Window   13

My Dead-Grandmother Essay   29

Scissors   42

Ghost Siblings   49

Garbage-Bag Charity   57

At His Feet as Dead   73

Give 'Em Jesus   97

Hot Girls in Short Skirts   111

Shake Terribly the Earth   130

November Leaves   154

Boat Stories: Three Generations   157

The *Tricia* Has Crashed   170

Kite String   188

family tree

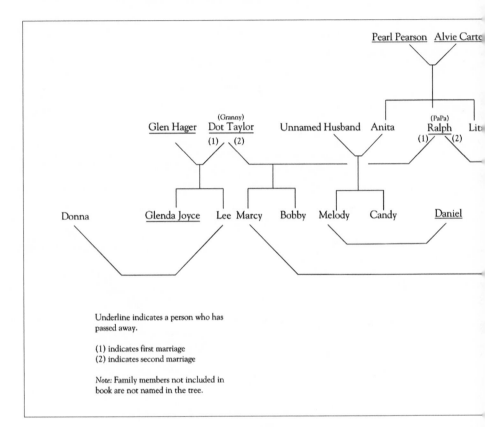

Pearl Pearson   Alvie Carter

(Granny)
Glen Hager   Dot Taylor   Unnamed Husband   Anita   (PaPa) Ralph   Lit
(1)   (2)   (1)   (2)

Donna   Glenda Joyce   Lee   Marcy   Bobby   Melody   Candy   Daniel

Underline indicates a person who has
passed away.

(1) indicates first marriage
(2) indicates second marriage

Note: Family members not included in
book are not named in the tree.

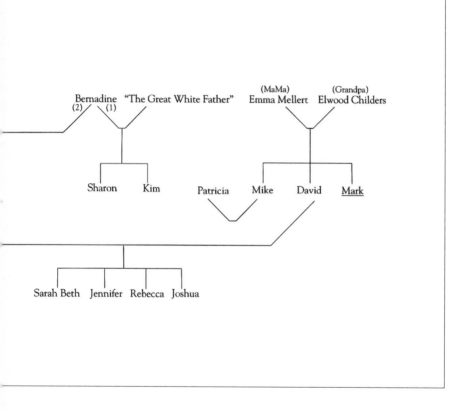

O Glorious Love

WHEN I WAS A LITTLE GIRL, THE MOST important musicians in my life were John Denver and a Methodist minister named Keith Leap. I listened to them equally—John Denver on the living room record player, Keith Leap on a locally produced cassette tape my parents had purchased from Leap himself.

I thought both men were handsome. John Denver had the same big glasses my daddy wore, and Keith Leap had heavy sideburns and fascinating clothes. On the cassette's cardboard insert, the minister smiled benignly in a tan plaid jacket and a wide, robin egg-tint necktie. I had no reason to believe that either of my two singers was better than the other. If someone had asked me, I might have said I preferred Keith Leap. His voice was rich and sonorous as a cloudless night sky.

My mother had seen both of my artists in person, so I often requested the stories. At a John Denver concert at the Huntington Civic Center, the singer had joked about how bad the local drinking water tasted. He'd played all our favorite songs—"Country Roads," "Calypso," "Annie's Song"—and my dad's shy little brother had danced like crazy when Denver sang "Thank God I'm a Country Boy." My mother had heard Keith Leap sing at a local Baptist church, and, after the service, she'd shaken his hand and bought his tape. "He looks just like the picture," she said. I smiled to myself, imagining these encounters with musical genius.

When my mother, Marcy, was fifteen years old, she got born again by listening to the radio. Her parents had been divorced for three years, and she lived with her mother, Dot, who sulked and smoked on the black vinyl couch after work and forbade Marcy to use her washing machine. When Dot repeated her favorite threat—"You'll come home and find the door locked and your clothes out in the street"—Marcy found radio evangelists more comforting than the top forty station.

One of Marcy's favorites was Jimmy Swaggart, back in his preadultery days. Taking inspiration from his sinful first cousin, Jerry Lee Lewis, Reverend Swaggart preached the evils of rock and roll along with redemption. A talented pianist himself, the reverend took pride in keeping his wayward fingers on a leash. He performed only the most church-appropriate flourishes and chords. Moved by Swaggart's sermons, Marcy smashed her record collection and kept her radio tuned to a station that played only preachers and hymns.

I grew up in the late '80s and '90s, but I have no memory of the musicians of that era. While other children bought New Kids on the Block T-shirts and hid Nirvana cassettes in their underwear drawers, my two sisters and I cheered when the soft-voiced radio announcer played our favorite hymns. "To God Be the Glory" and "He Arose!" were my hymns of choice. "To God Be the Glory" had an upbeat, singable melody, and the account of Christ's death and resurrection in "He Arose!" was triumphant enough to give me goose bumps. We made do with what with we had, and we were happy.

But even though I could appreciate the hymns station as a little girl, I knew those church choirs and Sunday morning soloists weren't serious artists. When I needed to hear some real music, I asked my mother to root out the Keith Leap cassette or one of the John Denver records that had survived the music purge of her youth. She'd made an exception for Denver because she loved him. He sang about the mountains, roads, and moonshine of our home state, West Virginia.

I needed some real music one evening on the way home from visiting Dot, my granny. We ate dinner at Granny's house every Thursday, and her food was tastier, and greasier, than anything my mother ever fixed. Chicken fried in Crisco, saltine-coated flounder, macaroni and cheese layered with butter and canned milk. When Granny was doing well, she showed up at the door in a neat polyester pantsuit, ushering us into the kitchen through a cloud of cigarette smoke. When she was doing badly, she wore a pink nightgown and forgot to cook.

One night, Granny fixed fried chicken, but she came to the door in the nightgown. We smiled and drank our iced tea like everything was normal, but she started screaming at my mother during the meal. My mom pulled my chair out from the table and grabbed the baby. "Go out and get in the car *now*," she hissed. My dad had bolted first; he already had the motor running. One more glance at Granny—her wild black hair, her eyes glaring at me like I was a roach that needed squashing—and I ran for the car. My mother had to sneak back inside for my shoes.

On the car ride home, I wept silently for a few minutes, then I said, "Put on Keith Leap." I snuggled down into my booster seat and squeezed my Cabbage Patch doll as my dad turned up the volume. "O glorious love of Christ my Lord divine!" Leap's voice rumbled from the speakers like floodwater through a dam, filling up the car to the chocolate-stained ceiling.

+ + +

DURING dessert one year at the Pearson family reunion, a man stood up and sang. In the reunion's former days, the Pearsons themselves had done the singing, gathered around a battered piano in a corner of the rented community room. A middle-aged distant relative banged out rousing melodies like "I'll Fly Away," and my great-aunts and second cousins kept time with their canes. The best singer by far was Dot's ex-husband, my PaPa Ralph, who closed his eyes and bellowed like he was standing alone at the front of a church.

By the year the man sang, Ralph and many of the cane-tappers had already flown away, and the reunion organizers hired local southern gospel groups for our after-dinner entertainment. While we piled green beans onto our paper plates, a clean-shaven man in an Oxford shirt and a few women with teased hair set up their amp and speakers. They placed a modestly short stack of their latest recording next to the reunion photo albums, ready for purchase.

I was a teenager then, and I'd rejected hymns—those solemn melodies penned by long-buried reverends—in favor of Christian rock. I'd absorbed enough of my mother's holy streak to steer clear of real rock stars, but I loved those jeans-wearing, guitar-playing, messy-haired performers who grinned from the pages of Christian music magazines. I considered southern gospel one dull step above hymns, and I usually escaped outdoors with my dad during the reunion performances. But this year was different: the southern gospel group included a blond teenage boy. I liked blond, male Christian rockers, even the ones with scratchy voices and goofy lyrics, so I figured I'd give this group a shot.

But then, while the singers were testing their microphones and the Pearsons were still loading cobbler onto their dessert plates, a man stood up in front of his folding chair. He had a prominent mole on his large nose, and his untucked shirt had a greasy stain. To my teenage eyes, this man looked repulsive, more like a cobbler-devouring Pearson than a vocalist whose music I'd buy on CD. "I'm your dear sister Rita's pastor," he explained, motioning toward the beaming elderly woman in the seat beside him. "She asked me to sing 'Beulah Land' for you all."

The man paused while a few uncles shuffled to their seats, and then he closed his eyes and sang. He launched his unaccompanied baritone into that linoleum-tiled room, and I realized this was the way the song was meant to be sung. A pure expression of the spirit. The man's voice sliced through my teenage trendiness-worship and touched the part of me that had loved Keith Leap when I was a little girl. I felt sorry for the southern gospel group after that. At least one Pearson no longer cared to hear them.

After the song ended, the man confided, "When I think of that song, I think of my mother." The elderly female audience chuckled with approval. Then he told us a story. The night his mother died, he drove her to the hospital, surrounding her emaciated body with pillows in the backseat of his station wagon. The road was long, winding, and potholed, and every bump jolted agony through her bones. "Honey," she gasped, "sing 'Beulah Land.'" Her son's voice filled the car, and she imagined herself already in heaven.

✦ ✦ ✦

IN moments of profound sorrow or disquiet, I sometimes find myself replaying that Keith Leap tape in my head. I close my eyes and imagine every note as Leap sang it; when he hits the high notes, I hold my breath. "O glorious love of Christ my Lord divine! That made Him stoop to save a soul like mine." The words themselves calm me, I'm sure, but it's not only the words. If I try to hum the song in my own weak voice, the spell is broken. So it seemed preternaturally fitting when Keith Leap himself preached and *sang* at Dot's funeral a few years ago.

On a bright July day, Dot fell beside the bathtub and landed in the hospital. Her mind didn't go with her. When I visited her hospital room, she thought we were sitting at her kitchen table. She shook a finger toward her refrigerator, telling me to get myself a can of 7UP. My cousin came to visit, and suddenly she and Granny were in a dark alley, crouching under blankets in a truck bed. Rain pounded the thin wool, and the truck rocked with every crash of thunder. Somewhere in the darkness, a rapist lurked. "We have to get out of the truck," Granny wailed. "We have to get across the street." Granny had received messages from her toaster in the past, but she'd always been able to live alone. The doctors told us she was dying.

We were sad, but my mother's chief worry was finding someone to preach the funeral. My family hadn't been to church in several years, choosing to pray at home on Sunday mornings. Dot hadn't been to church in three decades; she'd left her Methodist church about the same time she'd stopped working. I wonder if God existed for my grandmother in pieces of remembered hymns.

My mother called Paul, a licensed minister friend she'd known since her teenage years, and he said he'd love to help out. "I'll even buzz by your mother's room, be a pastor to her," Paul said. He never did buzz by, and he backed out completely on the night she died. "Funerals make me nervous," he said. I wonder if Paul sat down to compose his sermon and remembered my parents' wedding shower. Dot had shown up with unwashed hair, offering a stack of flyspecked recipe cards.

When my mother hung up the phone and sat down to cry, my dad had an inspiration. He'd heard somewhere that Keith Leap had accepted the pastorate at Dot's old church. *Keith Leap!* My dad found the church's number in the Yellow Pages, and my mom called. The minister answered the phone himself. My sisters and I hovered in the background, in our twenties but still giggly. My mom covered the mouthpiece and told us he'd do it.

I whispered, "'O Glorious Love'!"

"And would you mind singing 'O Glorious Love'?"

Of course he didn't mind singing. What surprised us was Keith Leap's sincere joy at the prospect of preaching a stranger's funeral at the last minute. "I won't take a penny," he told my mother on the phone. "She's a church member, and I don't charge members of Highlawn Methodist." He was doing my family no favors: he was preaching this funeral for Dot. To me, he seemed to regard my granny as a bruised, dirty, and cigarette-smelling sheep, returned to his fold at last.

Dot's viewing happened to fall on the day of the Pearson reunion, so we grieved in a crowd. After the last cobbler crumbs had disappeared and that year's southern gospel group had loaded their speakers back into their minivan, the Pearsons descended on the funeral home. They had been Dot's in-laws before her and Ralph's divorce, but they were there to support my mother, not Ralph's nutty first wife. Dot lay forgotten in the corner as her guests yarned and joked. I stood by Granny for a while, keeping her company, then I gave up and sat down next to Ralph's sister Anita. In between stories about her own days as a vaudeville dancer in Kansas City, my great-aunt confided she'd "never had any problem with Dot."

Keith Leap hovered around the gathering's edges in a black suit, armed with a Bible and a handshake. His hair had gone gray and his wide tie had shrunk, but Keith Leap he certainly was. He paid his respects beside the casket and contemplated the picture collage: Dot as a dark-haired mother with Cherokee eyes and white gloves, Dot as a smiling grandmother with a turquoise blouse and baby on her hip. "What a beautiful woman," he remarked. Dot *was* beautiful, even at eighty-two. Seeing only the photos and a body at peaceful rest, the minister could imagine a woman remarkable not for her mind, but her beauty. Dot wasn't there to make him forget it.

By the day of the funeral, the Pearsons had all gone home, leaving only Dot's three children and her small swarm of grandchildren and great-grandchildren to fill the pews in the funeral home chapel. Dot had driven away all of her friends long before, and most of them were dead by then anyway. Even some of Dot's own descendants hadn't always been willing to brave her company, and the tiniest of the group had never met her until my cousin lugged her children into the room where Dot died. "Kiss your granny," my cousin had said, pointing to the half-conscious woman, her dentures in a labeled Ziploc on the nightstand, her features flattened and gray.

My grandparents on my dad's side filled two spots on a pew, though they'd barely seen Dot since my parents' wedding. They'd pulled their funeral garb from the clothes they wore to the Baptist church every Sunday: Grandpa in a gray wool suit, MaMa in pale blue, her blond curls fresh from her neighbor's basement salon. My sisters, my brother, and I gave up our seats to our cousins and sat in the back with MaMa and Grandpa, the only grandparents we had left. I shuddered when MaMa tucked a brochure for prepaid funerals into her handbag.

Leap's sermon was nothing special: an eloquent treatise on flower-like grandmothers that had little relevance to Granny. But then he put down his Bible, he pushed *Play* on a boom box, and he sang. "O glorious love of Christ my Lord divine!" His voice burst through the stale funeral air, and the funeral chapel transformed into an ordinary room. I was attending a live performance by a singer I'd loved for years.

I'd dragged my family to Christian rock concerts, where we'd purchased seats just two rows from the amped-up drums and guitars. And I'd heard plenty of talented vocalists at church. But except for that singing preacher at the Pearson reunion, I'd never heard a performance like this. Before Leap sang, I'd feared age might have weakened his vocal chords, but his voice sounded fuller and richer than it did on the tape. And I could see his eyebrows lift and his chest swell as he declared: "My song will silence never! I'll worship Him forever! And praise Him for His glorious love."

Listening to Keith Leap, I was a little girl holding a Cabbage Patch doll in my parents' backseat. But this time my granny wasn't alone in her house, quivering as she lit a fresh cigarette. She was free of her body and diseased mind, really well for the first time in decades.

Leap's song soared through the chapel's cheap stained-glass windows and into the bread factory across the street, his voice mingling with the warm, yeasty scent. When he finished, MaMa leaned over to me and whispered, "That was so beautiful I could hardly stand it."

Shorn

TOOK A WALK WITH MY PAPA RALPH ONE spring afternoon when I was five. Because of his heart condition, PaPa walked often, thumping along the brick streets with his prosthetic leg and metal cane. PaPa seemed old to me then, but he was only sixty-two; dark hair still covered his head.

On that walk, PaPa and I clutched each other's hands as we plodded past a gaping pothole, an unsteady blue house with a jungle of weeds, and a driveway that seemed to angle straight up into a thatch of maples. I held PaPa's hand believing he needed me for balance; he held mine to keep me from skipping off down the street.

I'd been able to read badly since I was three and well since I was four, and PaPa was proud of his first grandchild. He showcased his tiny reader for visiting cousins, handing me *National Geographic* and gloating as I sounded out articles about the Nyangatom people and Kentucky caves. As we walked, PaPa pointed out road signs, business signs, names on mailboxes, and angry poster boards nailed to shabby porches. He bellowed, "Read that one, Doll!" And I read. TWENTY-NINTH STREET. GINO'S PIZZA. THE MAYOR IS A CROOK.

We stopped for a root beer in TED'S IMPERIAL LANES, a prospect I found exciting because my parents refused to take me. The inside was less spectacular than I'd hoped: a dim bowling alley full of loud, greasy-haired people with cigarettes. I clung closer to PaPa's polyester polo as he bought our root beer and chose a table with two sticky vinyl chairs. When PaPa sat, he crossed his fake leg over his real one and straightened his sock; the white nylon had slipped down the flesh-colored plastic. Then he asked me to read the names on the scoreboards.

On the way back to PaPa's, we ambled past SANSOM'S USED CARS, and the name intrigued me. *Sansom.* So close to *Samson,* the hero in my Bible storybook, drawn with seven long black locks and muscles that bulged under his dark red tunic. Early in Samson's story, he snarls in the picture, fists outstretched, gripping the dry jawbone of a donkey he's used to slay a thousand Philistines. Bodies litter the sandy earth around his sandals. In a later picture, after his run-in with Delilah, Samson's hair is short and ragged, his eyes empty bruises. Feasting Philistines in gold rings and purple cloaks mock Samson as he stands, chained to stone pillars that support the house where the laughing people sit. The Philistines should have known this was a bad idea. Samson bows his head, so shamefully bare, and prays for the strength to kill himself with the Philistine lords.

PaPa died three years after that walk, and when I think about him, I often think of our journey to the bowling alley: I'm alone and happy with PaPa, who is as healthy as I ever saw him. And in this memory, that sign for Sansom's car lot burns as clearly as PaPa's shiny cane, his striped polo shirt, his wavy dark hair. And behind that sign lurks a drawing of Samson. I wonder why I remember that sign so clearly—if, as a five-year-old, I connected the two fiery, dark-haired men. Both of them robbed of their might. With PaPa's left leg a dead thing he propped in a bedroom corner when he slept, he barely seemed the same man as that robust father in my mother's photo album, the teenage sailor in his sisters' stories, who had battled the Japanese in the South Pacific.

But I didn't think of PaPa as weak. I squeezed his hand in dingy alleys because he needed me; deprived of his sight, even Samson needed a child to guide his hands to the stone pillars. And I clung to PaPa because I depended on him. If a greasy person had crept after us out of that bowling alley, PaPa would have defended me with his cane if he had to, summoning his former strength with a prayer.

Through a Train Window

URING THE GREAT DEPRESSION, WHEN my PaPa Ralph was a little boy, he raced his sisters down the street to meet the daily trains in Peach Creek, West Virginia. Alvie, Ralph's father and my mother's grandfather, served as the town's postmaster general. The job came with a home for his wife and six children: a three-room apartment above the small brick post office.

Every morning, while Alvie sorted letters downstairs and his wife Pearl stirred a pot and fed the baby, little Ralph and a few of his sisters poked their heads out of the upstairs front window. They stomped each other's toes and watched a distant hillside for a cloud of gray smoke. The kid who spotted it first got to yell, "Mother! The train is coming, the train is coming!"

Pearl handed the oldest girl a parcel of outgoing mail and put a firm hand on her head. "Don't get yourselves killed in the street."

The children walked a few steps, away from their mother's eyes at the window. Ralph yelled, "I'll beat you girls *and* that train!" The fastest runner got to gloat on the wooden platform for a few minutes before the train rolled into the station. When the train arrived, the children handed over the parcel and accepted a sack of letters, postcards, and bills they'd distribute to the good folks of Peach Creek.

During World War II, Alvie landed a job as a railroad conductor, and he moved his family to a two-story house in

Huntington, West Virginia, with mustard-colored siding, three bedrooms, and a backyard. Pearl got a cat, Ralph dropped out of high school and joined the navy, and the younger girls danced with soldiers at the VFW. The older girls were already married, the eldest sister to the philandering owner of Peach Creek's grocery store. Anita, a girl who looked like the blondes in the Pepsi-Cola ads, had moved across the country with husband number two.

As a conductor, Alvie commanded from the caboose, testing the train's brakes, caring for passengers, ordering the engineer to start the engine or slow down, and keeping a log of the journey. I wish I could read one of Alvie's logs, see his handwriting in a notebook, the relics of his thoughts. I wonder if he kept the log clean and professional, recording only the times the train stopped and started and problems with the engine and track. Or might he have jotted a message to himself? *Need to buy a jar of jelly for Pearl at the Huntington station. Just saw a robin carrying a worm into a bush—must be a nest.* If I kept a conductor's log, I know daydreams would creep in: descriptions of the countryside, a sweetheart at home, places I'd rather be.

I never met Alvie. He died a few years before I was born, passing unexpectedly after what had seemed like a relatively harmless topple down the stairs. My mother has a picture of Alvie in middle age. In the photograph, he looks long and lanky, almost delicate, and his high forehead lengthens his thin, serious face. Perhaps a man with a face that serious wouldn't use his conductor's log as a diary. One of Alvie's arms drapes around Pearl; thick coils of braids cover her ears. Pearl said Alvie sulked for three days after she cut off her hair.

Pearl, my great-grandmother, did live until I could meet her. I remember her sitting on a worn-out couch in the mustard-colored house, wearing a red-and-purple sweatsuit. She cradled the dolls I brought to show her, admiring their dresses and curls through hazel eyes emptied by Alzheimer's. But her mind was still clear enough to tell a story: her midwife mother who rode a horse around southern West Virginia, delivering babies on blood-soaked beds; her daring little-girl self jumping off a barn with only an umbrella to break her fall; her conductor husband who could procure free train tickets for family trips.

"The conductor is the most important man on a train," she told me proudly, smoothing my doll's dress with her rumpled hand. "He kept all those passengers safe."

Across the room, Ralph chuckled in his white leather chair. He'd moved back home after he'd had a heart attack and retired from his own railroad job, and his second wife had thrown him out. "I was just an engineer," he said, "so I'm chopped liver."

"What's that man laughing for?" Pearl demanded, and she told me about Alvie all over again.

+ + +

SEVERAL years ago, I took a train trip across southern West Virginia and back, just for the joy of the ride. I'd never ridden a train before, and I wanted to view my autumn-brown state through the pane above my seat. Muddy brooks, unpainted barns, hillsides of sticks with scattered, clinging leaves. On the train, I pulled my knees against my chest and stared out the window. I imagined the passing red maples covered first in tiny scarlet spring blossoms, then in serrated emerald leaves that reddened—painting the trees scarlet again—before they blew across the tracks and snagged on the rails. I daydreamed about Ralph and Alvie, who'd spent half their lives on trains.

I'm sure I stared too long at the conductor when he checked my ticket. Unlike my balding great-grandfather, this conductor had thick white hair under a hat that matched his dark blue suit. He smiled at me and bowed slightly, offering information about food in the club and dining cars. I imagined Alvie's face on the conductor's body, trying to picture that solemn man in the photograph with his eyes lit up by a smile.

I didn't see the engineer on the trip, tucked away in the front like an airplane pilot, so I imagined Ralph was driving. I pictured a strong man in his forties, his dark hair covered by a red polka-dot engineer cap my mother had told me he often wore. "It makes me nauseous just to think about that ugly hat," my mother had said with a shudder.

As he drove my train through the mountains, Ralph whistled a Hank Williams tune and thought about his children back at home, playing in the creek.

+ + +

I'D like to think Ralph wished as a boy to become an engineer, imagining himself inside the trains as they pulled into the Peach Creek station. But I know he did it for the money. Ralph dreamed of a career as a radio DJ. He had a passion for country-western music—"Back in the Saddle Again" by Gene Autry, Roy Acuff's version of "Wabash Cannonball"—and he wanted to decide when his favorite songs got played. "Luckies are always smooth, mild, and mellow, every puff of the way," Ralph intoned to himself when alone.

Once, while Ralph was away in World War II, he mailed home a spoken message to his family, captured on a vinyl record. His parents and sisters hadn't heard Ralph's voice in over a year, so they gathered around the record player and played the message again and again, sighing impatiently through the advertisement for Pepsi-Cola, the project's sponsor. I don't know what Ralph said in that message, but I'm sure he took the recording seriously. I'd bet he practiced and practiced his stories and jokes, pretending he'd be heard on the radio all over the U.S. and imagining the sound of his sisters' laughter.

Then the war ended, and Ralph came home, restless and eager to work. After he tired of hugs and welcome-home pies, he needed to get out of the house. He suffered from shellshock—his mother and sisters had to wake him up with a broom handle for fear he'd attack them—and Pearl thought a job might help. Ralph chose to work for the railroad because his father had connections. Railroad jobs paid well and didn't require Ralph to go back to school and earn his high school diploma. You just had to work your way up. Ralph started out as a sweaty, coal-shoveling fireman. When the railroad abandoned steam for diesel, he stayed on as a fireman, a position that now meant "engineer's assistant." Finally, he moved up to engineer, with a salary that would allow him to buy a small house and marry a pretty woman who didn't work.

I have a letter Ralph wrote to his younger sister Lita in Huntington, not long after he'd begun working for the railroad. He was staying with his grocer's-wife sister in Peach Creek. Ralph doesn't mention the railroad, but he seems happy. It's obvious he saw his letter, like nearly every other moment of his life, as an opportunity to entertain. *Say! do you happen to know what a Hydromatic Hillbilly is*, Ralph writes. *He is a shiftless son of a bitch. Joke that is.* I'm sure Lita shook with laughter when she read about the death of an old Peach Creek acquaintance: *Do you remember the fellow we used to call Popeye? He would always stick his chin out when we called to him. He died day before yester-day.*

Finally, Ralph comes to the letter's point: *I have de-cided to buy myself a Birthday present.* The present? His first car, bought with money he'd saved from his railroad earnings.

But Ralph still hadn't forgotten the radio dream. After he'd worked a couple of years as an engineer, freezing in the winter, gripping the throttle through the night so the engine wouldn't stall, he saw a job ad for a position as a radio DJ. The local country station called Ralph for an audition, and he impressed the manager with his rich voice and quick wit. The station offered him the job, and he accepted immediately.

I picture Ralph in his late twenties, practically dancing out of that radio station. He opens the door and puts on his brown fedora, whistling to himself. He takes one step outside—one foot on the sidewalk, the job is his, he's ready to tell the railroad he's done — and then he stops. He takes his hat off and walks back to the manager's office. Flashing his boyish, crooked smile, as if what he has to say doesn't matter much, he asks, "By the way, how much does this job pay?" The man told him, and Ralph turned the job down. He was already making three times that salary driving trains.

Ralph strode back through the door and drove away in his car, the car he'd bought with his railroad money.

+ + +

WHEN I was little, Ralph took long, slow walks. He videotaped my siblings and me, waited in his front yard until cardinals ate from his hand, and watched *The Lawrence Welk Show* until Lawrence finished dancing and bid viewers *adios, au revoir, auf wiedersehen.* A few years before I was born, Ralph had lost his leg to gangrene after one of many heart surgeries, and he was taking his final years easy. The only remnants of his railroad days were his stories and his collection of memorabilia: C&O Chessie Cat dinner plates, model locomotives, mugs printed with Norman Rockwell's steaming railroad scenes.

When my mother was little, Ralph worked so much his family barely saw him. Instead of a regular salary, he got paid by the job, and he signed up to work as much as he could. When he was off work, he signed up to be on call.

My mom remembers a rare day when her father took a break: he drove her and her brothers to Dreamland, a local pool murky with the cigarettes parents had smoked while their children swam. For twenty minutes, Marcy and her brothers splashed around while Ralph relaxed on a towel, adding a few cigarette butts of his own and glancing slyly at the "slick legs," his term for pretty women. Then it was time for Ralph to head back to work. "Angel Pie," he called to Marcy, who was about to plunge headfirst down the slide, "we gotta go."

Marcy slid down feet first, sitting up—the slowest possible way—then trudged back to Ralph's towel. "Daddy, can we stay just a *little* longer?" she implored, her hair and swimsuit creating a puddle by Ralph's feet.

"Marcy, I have to work, or we'll end up in the poorhouse," he said, pulling his shirt back on over his swimming trunks.

I wonder if the "poorhouse" Ralph meant was the cramped apartment over the Peach Creek Post Office. Did he fear if he passed up one opportunity to earn money, his young family's house would disappear? Maybe so. When he wrote his name in every possible blank on the yard office bulletin board, I'm sure he believed he was grasping each moment of his life and giving those moments to his family. He didn't realize it was worth something to lie on a towel while his kids splashed around in the pool.

✦ ✦ ✦

THE same year I rode my first real train, I took a university course on the history of the American railroad. The course was taught by Cal, a jolly man with a curly white comb-over. He lived, on purpose, in a house that lay feet from a train track. In the evenings, he and his wife sat on their porch swing and watched the trains roll by. They felt the train's rumble in their shoes. "Usually we see coal trains, but *sometimes*," Cal told the class, his eyes widening, "we see one with passengers."

I found this sweet, amusing. To get to the university from my house, I had to cross seven tracks. Most mornings, I got trapped at least once behind a black wall of steel, coal, and graffiti. Still, I could sympathize with Cal. Tracks and passing locomotives reminded me of PaPa, and I knew my mom loved to watch trains.

When I was little, my mom seemed to enjoy getting stuck at railroad crossings on the morning drive to Grace Christian School. As the train rattled by, she told my siblings and me about the days when she'd ridden in the car with her mother to drop off her father at the yard. Red polka-dot cap on his head, a shiny silver lunch bucket in hand, Ralph had disappeared into the one-story cinderblock building to sign up for jobs and board the locomotives. Each locomotive had had its own raunchy nickname. "I only remember one name, and it's too disgusting to repeat," my mother told us.

After a few stories, she whipped out a cassette tape of "Wabash Cannonball," and, ignoring the creeping digital clock on the dash, we all sang about the mighty "rumble and the roar," nearly drowning out the noise of the real train in front of us.

One day during the railroad class, Cal took the students on a field trip to the Huntington Railroad Museum, a motley collection of old locomotives and cabooses in a small, tree-lined field. The cars, resting on short pieces of track and white gravel, reminded me of the red-and-black model locomotive PaPa had kept by his bed until he died.

A few middle-aged men, members of the Collis P. Huntington Railroad Society—named for the railroad magnate who named Huntington after himself—gave us a tour of the museum's displays. We stood in the field and listened to stories about a coal black steam locomotive from 1914, a modern diesel engine from the 1960s, and a shiny yellow caboose built in 1924 and updated in the late 1950s, at a time when Ralph rode the tracks.

Cal must have enjoyed talking with people who loved trains as much as he did, one of them sporting a striped engineer's cap. The men didn't share his optimism, however. The man in the hat gave his captive audience of slouching students a lecture about the railroad's most dangerous enemy: the U.S. government. "There's two-story Superliners, beautiful trains, out in the fields just rusting away," he said, nearly shouting. "And, next thing you know, they'll be shutting down Amtrak. Congress don't care *nothing* about trains."

"Well, we've got old Senator Byrd to watch out for us," Cal chirped, shaking a hopeful finger.

The museum worker punctuated his disdain with a stream of tobacco spit. "He's not *that* good."

Before the tour ended, we took turns boarding the train cars. First, I stood inside the steam locomotive and stared at the square black firebox. Empty and cold, the firebox seemed haunted by fire, low paychecks, and sweat. Since Ralph began his career as a fireman, I imagined him in his early twenties, handsome despite his heavy gloves, soot-covered overalls, and the weariness in his eyebrows. Again and again, my ghost-Ralph wielded his shovel, feeding coal to the flames.

The tour moved on to the caboose, where I climbed a short ladder and sat down in the cupola, the conductor's domain, a small upper compartment with windows for walls. Even standing still, the cupola felt peaceful. A place a philosopher might sit. After taking tickets and chatting with passengers, Alvie must have retired to a room like this one. Away from the chatting passengers, he could hear only the engine, the wheels on the tracks, the train whistle, tree branches scraping against the train cars. Alvie used this sanctuary to jot notes in his log, to watch the pink rays of sunrise on the creeks and rivers, and to look out for trouble: a tree trunk that had fallen across the tracks during a storm.

I felt most at home in the final train car I boarded, the diesel engine from the 1960s, when Ralph worked as an engineer. Holding up the line of students who wanted to finish the tour, I lingered in the engineer's seat. It was possible PaPa had sat in this very seat, long before the yellow foam had burst through the black vinyl. I fingered the round dials, the knobby brake handle, and the sideways lever that worked roughly like the gearshift in a standard transmission car. I wished I could wear that museum worker's striped blue hat, feel the sweaty canvas on my head as I looked through the windows, imagining trees whizzing by on both sides and end-less track ahead of me.

The vinyl seat, the lever, the controls: a new window into PaPa's life. In Ralph's seat, I could sense some of the power he must have felt as he controlled a massive engine with his hands, zooming along the train tracks. As I gripped the throttle, imag-ining myself thundering down the tracks, I realized something about Ralph. He worked all the time to make more money, but he also worked so much because it was *fun*. He loved the speed, the freedom, the beauty he saw through the train windows.

As Ralph drove his children home from the pool, Marcy and her brothers pointed their gloomy faces back toward the slides, shifting on the towels Ralph had placed under their bare legs so they wouldn't stick to the vinyl seats. Ralph stared straight ahead, his lips curled around a cigarette, his mind al-ready on the tracks, the rivers, the wind rustling in the leaves.

+ + +

I never saw PaPa driving a train, but I can imagine his engineer gusto from the way he drove his cars. A long white sedan with tiny black dots on the ceiling that blurred if you stared at them too long. Then a compact Plymouth Reliant with shiny white paint and exquisitely vacuumed upholstery.

Every day after kindergarten, PaPa rolled onto the school parking lot and leaned across the seat to open the side pas-senger door. "Get in, Doll," he said. "Let's get us something to eat." My parents trapped me in a sweaty booster seat in the backseat, next to my sleeping baby sister, but PaPa let me sit in front with him, my bottom and unbent legs right against the soft burgundy upholstery. Inside the car, I peered around his brown tweed coat and studied the circles and needles on the dashboard, as mysterious to me as the gauges on a locomotive.

Cane in the backseat, PaPa sped around town with the confidence of a man who had made his living by driving. He

ignored traffic laws and glided over bumpy brick streets. Usually, PaPa zipped straight to the mustard-colored house. His sister Anita, who had moved back home after her long series of
divorces, fixed us sauerkraut and hotdogs.

But sometimes, PaPa felt a little less thrifty. He knew the
fastest routes to McDonald's, Jim's Spaghetti House, and
Captain D's. In the drive-thru, he'd crank down his window
and bellow his order into the microphone, using a deep, reso-
nant voice he saved for his occasional sermons at the Methodist church, lengthy orations at family reunions, and fast food
orders in drive-thrus. "Give me the senior citizen discount," he
said proudly. With those two words, *senior citizen,* I'm sure PaPa
meant to tell those hush puppy fryers what an important cus-
tomer they were serving, a man who deserved a discount. He'd
survived the Depression, fought the world's greatest war, and
he'd come home and worked like crazy. At the time, I couldn't
understand any of this, but I took pride in the pride in my
PaPa's voice. I felt like I was riding with a king.

Greasy bag in tow, PaPa hurtled on home, never pausing
for a turn signal. When the car stopped, I jumped out and
hopped with impatience as he crept out of the car, one hand
leaning on the hood, the other gripping his cane.

✣   ✣   ✣

I'D been on trains before that trip across West Virginia, but
they weren't real. When I was little, my sisters and I created an
imaginary train out of the kitchen cabinets. After we tossed
the pots, pans, and recipe books onto the linoleum, we each
chose a train car, jamming ourselves and several dolls into
the cool, dark space. I yelled, "All a-*board!* Is everybody on
the train?" remembering my mother's words from when she'd
played train with me as a toddler, and imitating PaPa's voice:
deep, slow, strong, and tinged, like mine, with Appalachia.
Then, banging the wooden doors to show we were moving,

my sisters and I set off to places as exotic as we could imagine, like Indiana or Michigan.

I'd also ridden the less than real train at Camden Park, a century-old amusement park boasting an ancient log flume, a weed-covered Indian burial mound, and a shaky wooden roller coaster where a child once died from the bite of a copperhead that had stowed away under his seat. My mom's favorite park attraction was the life-sized train, so, to my annoyance, my family always ended our summer visits with a slow ride on its little loop of track.

Every year, I sulked quietly as we waited in line, frowning when my dad pulled me from my perch on the concrete barricade meant to protect children from being crushed under the train's wheels. I knew this would be the last ride of the day, and I wanted to spend it on the airplanes, cruising a few feet over the hot asphalt in a breezy circle, or in the cars, gripping a steering wheel as my tiny automobile careened around a racetrack. Oblivious to my exasperation, my mom stood in line behind me next to PaPa. She pushed the baby in a heat-sticky stroller, and PaPa leaned on his metal cane, teasing my mother until her ears turned red. "You're the prettiest woman in the park," he said. "Isn't that right, Sarah Beth?"

The train pulled in, a string of open-air cars labeled Dodge City, Cheyenne, and Santa Fe, railroad stops of the old West. Orange poles supported the cars' ceilings. Leaving the stroller with a ride attendant, we boarded, crowding onto two of the train's orange benches. I'm sure my mom smiled, looking at her daddy, her husband, her children, together, safe, and (for the most part) happy. The bells clanged, I cringed, and we set off on our adventure.

A small child's nightmare, that ride managed to combine boredom with terror. The train was painfully slow, crawling past the far speedier Hurricane and Tilt-a-Whirl and meandering through the middle of a Wild West drama. A few minutes into the ride, the train crept past a mannequin in a sunbonnet and a calico dress. She trembled in the doorway of a cabin, pressing her plastic baby to her chest. A train car's length ahead, an Indian in a feather headdress glared out of his black painted eyes, shaking his bloody tomahawk at the train. At five, I was certain that Indian would scalp me, or at least the mannequin and her baby. But cowboys in hats and bolo ties rescued us all, popping up behind a fence and firing their rifles at the Indians. Despite the cowboys' heroic role, I hated them even more than the Indians. Their gunshots assaulted my eardrums. At least the bloodthirsty Indian chief shook his tomahawk quietly. I buried my head in PaPa's lap, wishing the train had walls to protect us.

My mother insists I enjoyed the train one time I rode it. I was sixteen months old, too young to fear the Indians, and my mom must have covered my ears when the cowboys started shooting. I sat on her lap next to PaPa, clutching a big stuffed owl he'd won for me at the park. "That owl was bigger than you were," my mom tells me. To win the owl, PaPa had thrown hoops over the necks of glass milk jugs, spending twice as much money as the cost of a better owl at a toy store. By the time we rode the train, Styrofoam pellets were seeping through the owl's seams.

I enjoy this story when my mother tells it, more than I ever enjoyed a ride on that train. I like picturing myself happy with my grandfather. I realize now that spending time with his grandchildren was important to PaPa, that he wanted to make amends for his workaholic past. He'd been too busy for a day at the pool with his children, but he would brave an amusement park's heat, off-key music, and dirty tank tops to spend time with his daughter's little girl. And it wasn't enough to buy cotton candy and ride the train. He wasted money until he won me a junky toy.

I wish I'd kept that owl, though its beak had fallen off and its round white belly had grown flat and brown when my mom finally threw the bird away. That owl proves PaPa loved me. Throwing those hoops must have been exhausting. It wore him out to stand still for very long on his prosthetic leg, and I'm sure he felt an ache in his wallet far keener than the ache in his limbs.

The Great Depression permanently marked my grandfather, and his cheapness often overwhelmed his generosity. He paid for Marcy's wedding, but scrimped wherever he could; he paid less than $100 for a used wedding gown and he bought silk flowers when Marcy wanted real. Even worse, he humiliated his daughter by cutting a deal with the florist. Ralph asked if he could pour the homemade wax candles the store sold in exchange for a discount. The florist agreed, but he stared as Ralph bumbled around the half-bundled zinnias and sent him home after a few candles. "That man must have thought Daddy was dirt poor and felt sorry for him," my mom says, laughing now.

When Ralph became a grandfather, he began ordering a kid's meal when he went out for a hamburger. The food was cheap and came with a toy for his grandchildren. The toys in his stash were carefully rationed; he got angry when I reached for more than one. "Look at you, trying to steal a toy from your sisters and cousin. Do you want to send me to the poorhouse, Sarah Beth?" For PaPa, handing dollar after dollar to a teenager in a booth must have felt like a sacrifice.

But when I picture this scene—PaPa, me, and an owl on a train—I wonder what my grandfather was thinking. Would he have traded that wooden passenger bench for the black vinyl chair of an engineer? When PaPa looked out between the orange metal poles, I wonder if he saw what the rest of us did, children tugging their tired parents, warring mannequins, the back of the teacup ride. Or did he imagine what he used to see? Cornfields tucked between hills, fields full of mossy gravestones, falling pink blossoms and red and yellow leaves.

+ + +

I'VE considered seeking a railroad career, following in Ralph and Alvie's footsteps. I could work as an Amtrak conductor, punching tickets, lugging suitcases with my bony arms, staring out the window and keeping a log of my journey in a tea-stained notebook. Or I could get a job as a CSX engineer, crouching for days on a black vinyl seat, shuttling coal across West Virginia in open-topped freight cars. I've looked into it. The training is brief—a few intense weeks—and the pay high enough to be tempting. I meet the entrance qualifications, if only barely: steady hands, a sound mind, and the ability to lift forty pounds over my head.

I do worry I wouldn't survive the training. I envision myself on the first day, hunching nervously as I enter a classroom full of flannel shirts, Skoal cans, ball caps, and muscles, men from West Virginia and Kentucky who understand hard work. I'd feel small and out of place in a floral print skirt, with my too-perfect English. Probably I'd sneak back to my car and speed home during the first smoke break.

But what if I made it through? What if the railroad boiled up in my blood, and I understood what it means to love trains: the curving tracks through the front window, the rhythmic vibrations in my feet? Would I decorate my apartment with railroad mugs and work as much as I could? Would I give up on the goals I have now and focus only on the train track ahead of me?

My mom still regrets PaPa's unfulfilled dream of becoming a radio DJ. "It was that Depression mentality," she says sadly. "He should have been on the radio. All that man did was entertain. But all he could think about was money."

It's true that PaPa lived to entertain. When someone died at his church, he felt a secret excitement, hoping he'd get to sing at the funeral. At family reunions, he'd monopolize the conversation at his table, and he'd stand up and take over the whole room for thirty minutes, imitating the voices of long dead aunts. He even used his leg amputation as fodder for humor. On the phone with his sister Lita, he ticked off his list of Christmas gifts: "A calendar. A robe. One house shoe." Marcy, sitting next to her father's bed, could hear her aunt's laughter through the phone.

I wish Ralph had spent more time with my mother when she was little, but I don't think he needed to be a DJ. I think Ralph fulfilled his entertainment dream, just telling his jokes to his family.

+ + +

RALPH retired from the railroad at fifty-four. He was down to one good leg and at risk for another heart attack. Still, the railroad hated to lose such a dedicated worker. They gave him a rare and generous offer: part-time work during the day. He thought it over. During his illness, he'd watched way too much *Dallas* and *20/20*. It would be nice to get away from his second wife's evil dogs. He did miss that money. But Ralph decided at last to stay at home, and he packed away the polka-dot hat.

My mom says she understands her father's decision. After his heart attack, he tired easily, and he feared he couldn't handle even limited hours on a train. I'm sure she's right, but I wonder if physical weakness was his only reason.

When Ralph had his heart attack, his only daughter was about to get married with her silk flowers and hand-me-down dress. Ralph may have seen with new clarity as he learned to walk on that plastic leg so he could walk Marcy down the aisle. Grandchildren would soon be on their way. The doctors had told Ralph he might not have long to live, and he didn't want to spend that time on a train.

PaPa quit the railroad, and picked me up from kindergarten, and drove me to Captain D's for a snack.

My Dead-Grandmother Essay

*M*y Grandmother's Soft, Sweet Smell

When Granny felt fancy, she doused herself in *Interlude,* an amber perfume smelling of spice and molding flowers. I know the perfume's scent from sniffing the bottle; wearing it, Granny smelled only of cigarettes. Driving Granny to the store, I'd crank open a window, but my sinuses still closed.

Granny smoked in her house with the windows shut. She appeared to us in a cloud. Her walls had turned brown, and a romantic print of children by a lake a dull yellow. Nicotine crept through the cracks around her thin front door, darkening the edges and frame. We smelled Granny before we even knocked. All her food tasted blackened. Sipping her sweet tea, I detected nicotine in the ice cubes.

After Granny died, I asked my mother for one of her dressers. I needed furniture for my apartment, and I wished to own a piece of my grandmother's life. She'd had the same bedroom suite for over forty years, keeping her cash, her will, her deck of Uno cards, and her gun nestled among her underwear. So, my family scrubbed down a dresser and put it in our storage building for a few months, letting it air out with the garden tools, bicycles, and mice. Then my dad loaded the dresser into the family minivan and drove it all the way across West Virginia.

As he carried in the drawers, gently propping them against my clean white walls, I smelled a faint stench. I knew immediately I couldn't use the dresser. My sweaters would absorb Granny's smell; my head would hurt and friends would assume I'd taken up the wicked habit. Disappointed and sheepish, I asked him to load the dresser back up and drive it the four hours home.

Cherished Visits to Her Home

To see Granny, we drove thirty minutes to Guyandotte, West Virginia. Guyandotte is an old section of Huntington notable for its seedy bars, nineteenth-century churches, and an enthusiastic reenactment of the day a woman stopped the Union Army from burning her house by barricading herself and her children in the kitchen. Granny's bungalow sat on one of dozens of brick streets lined with small, crumbling dwellings that housed elderly women, shabby families, and rough-looking bachelors with pit bulls. We visited Granny often. She kept her phone unplugged, fearing unknown callers and aiming to annoy my mother. Visiting her house was the only way to check up on her.

We stood on the porch and knocked, watching for almond-shaped hazel eyes through the blinds, waiting for her to undo her five locks. When I was little we did our waiting on a porch of rotting blue wood; neighbors' cats hid in a hole in the corner. Later, my mom had the porch replaced with a slab of white concrete. After a silent minute, we'd knock again, louder, and I'd yell, "Granny, it's us! We came to see you."

If Granny was happy, she'd knock back from the inside, imitating the rhythm of our knocking. If she needed something, she'd hurry through her locks, throw open the door, and smile at my mother, declaring, "Blessed be the tie that binds!" If Granny was angry—or if my mom was sick and had sent my dad alone—she wouldn't open the door.

When my whole family visited Granny, my dad took walks down the narrow alleys, admiring neighbors' dogs through backyard fences and breathing the fresh air. Inside the house, my mother sat on the black vinyl couch in the living room and paid Granny's bills, the front door open despite Granny's protests. My siblings and I followed Granny back to a tiny sitting room, its shag-carpeted floor crammed with sagging recliners, a TV with rabbit ears, and a sewing machine table covered with clothes she'd bought too large on purpose so she could cut them down and sew them up smaller. We sank into the recliners, gathered around a card table thick with Yahtzee scorecards. Granny talked constantly, teaching us about life in between rattles of the dice.

Granny's lessons often amused us. She'd shake a long thin finger and insist that buying pantyhose would "steal food from our children's mouths." If a woman bought two pairs of thigh-high stockings and a garter belt, that'd be the only "leg coverings" she'd ever need. In her darker moods, she advised us all not to grow up like our mom, "an ungrateful gadabout who steals her mother's money." She excoriated our relatives, especially her ex-mother-in-law, "that damn Pearl Carter," to the day she died. Granny blamed our great-grandmother for her divorce from our PaPa Ralph.

Before we left, Granny often produced a shopping list written in her shaky black scrawl: groceries, Milk of Magnesia, gumdrops, black slip-on shoes. She would have asked for cigarettes, but my mom refused to buy them, so she shanghaied one of my mom's brothers or walked herself to the local drugstore where she bought them by the carton.

Often, my family drove to the store without Granny, enjoying a respite from the hot, smoky air. But sometimes she wanted to go out. She'd settle into the front passenger seat, her black vinyl purse in her lap. We were glad to see Granny getting out of the house, but we cringed at the thought of Granny in public. She might ask me if I needed underpants as we stood in line at a department store, or she might refuse to walk across a parking lot until a "colored man" had gotten into his car. Or she might mention that her toaster had whispered to her that her next-door neighbor was molesting her grandchildren. And she was certain to call the cashiers "sweetie," regardless of age or gender, confiding to them the troubles of being a "poor elderly woman." We learned to laugh at Granny. What else could we do?

For one trip to the grocery store, Granny bundled up in an ancient coat, her gray hair tied up in a crocheted navy head scarf. My mom whispered, "Mother, take those things off. You look like a Russian peasant."

"It doesn't matter what we wear, Marcy," Granny retorted loudly, sauntering past customers who looked up from the apples, curious. "We're not trying to put on a show." But Granny always put on a show. Loaded with Prednisone after an eye surgery, she danced in the cookie aisle, twirling and tapping to music only she could hear.

When we got back to the house, we'd put away her groceries and say our good-byes. If the visit ended happily, she'd kiss our cheeks and offer bags of candy, insisting my mother take a twenty for gas. Visits sometimes ended badly: she'd scream at my mother, demanding my mother's name be taken off her checks, or that her bank account be emptied so she could hide the money in her drawer. When my mother refused, Granny would stick out her wrinkled hands and lightly push her daughter, growling, "There's the door."

My Grandmother's Loving Bond with Her Daughter

Marcy devoted her youth to her mother. She turned down a scholarship to a seminary in Kentucky and went to Marshall University in Huntington. As Dot's only daughter, the duty fell on her to keep her mother from feeling alone. Marcy's older brother Lee had left for Vietnam when she was eleven, and he lived on an army base in Alabama for a few years when he came back. A year after Marcy gave up her scholarship, her younger brother Bobby joined the navy straight out of high school, traveling to Scotland on a submarine.

In the months before Bobby left, Dot's mental illness worsened. She was a surgical nurse, and she obsessed over the hospital's head of surgery, believing he would leave his wife and marry her. (We found his decade-old obituary—he'd died at eighty—tucked into Granny's wallet when she died.) Soon, Dot quit going to work and smoked on the couch all day. Marcy paid the bills and bought groceries with her part-time earnings from a department store and the money Bobby sent home from the navy. Sometimes Marcy sat on the wooden porch steps, counting change, calculating the cost of milk and cigarettes.

It had to have been hard on Marcy to live alone with Dot through her late teens and early twenties. With the washing machine off limits, Marcy washed her peasant blouses and bell-bottoms in the kitchen sink and hung them to dry, board-stiff, over the furnace. When Marcy expected a call from a friend, Dot turned off the phone. When I was little, I stared in awe at the patch on Granny's living room wall where my petite mother had punched a hole in frustration.

Dating increased the frustration. When boys picked up Marcy, she feared what Dot would say, and what her date would think. One boy, a Marshall University grad student and a future professor at a Fundamentalist Baptist college, thought the solution was obvious: "Put her in the state hospital, Marcy. Get her committed. It's not your fault you have a crazy mother." He smiled sympathetically through his bottle-bottom lenses. Marcy shuddered. She'd seen the local state hospital, the sterile white rooms, the mentally retarded children gathered around a television set.

When Marcy met David, my dad, she was impressed Dot didn't scare him away. Once, when they were dating, David fixed Dot's toilet while Marcy was at school. As he worked, wedged beside the bathtub, his hand in cold water in the porcelain tank, Dot accused him of plotting to steal the deed to her home. "I'll never go back there," he told Marcy on the phone. He did go back, but I don't think he ever enjoyed a conversation with Dot. A few years before she died, I watched Granny repeat her old accusation as my dad fixed her mailbox at my mother's request.

"You're wanting to steal this house for your own," Granny snapped, hovering behind my dad's shoulder on the porch, forgetting to hand him the glass of 7UP she'd brought out with her. "Otherwise, you wouldn't be so eager to fix it up." I admired his fortitude, that he didn't hurl the rusty metal over the brown concrete floodwall beside Granny's house and drive away.

After Marcy met David, she was grateful for his support, but things were getting desperate. Dot stood in the street, hair unwashed, trying to sell her vinyl couch to the neighbors for cigarette money. Feeling helpless, Marcy called her brothers, hoping they'd help her keep their mother at home. They regret it now, I'm sure, but they told Marcy to have her put away. Marcy rode the city bus to the state hospital and filled out the forms.

The police came for Dot while Marcy was at work, selling blouses to women with freshly teased hair. Marcy hadn't thought through what those forms meant, picturing herself gaining the courage to drive her mother out to the hospital herself, accompanied by a relative maybe, or David, or a friend, or perhaps forgetting the whole ordeal and leaving everything as it was. An officer called Marcy at work, informing her that her mother wouldn't let them in. "Miss Carter," he said, "we'll need your permission to break down the door."

Marcy screamed, "No!" She dropped a blouse, thinking of her mother, huddled against the back wall of the kitchen, shaking, confused and afraid.

Just hearing this story terrifies me. I picture Granny, un-washed, with unkempt hair in a pink nylon nightgown: the way she looked on her sickest days. And I picture her when she was happy, almost well, with red lipstick, a neat perm, and black polyester dress pants. I understand why my mom had to keep her at home.

Soon after Marcy told the police to leave, a lawyer held a hearing in Dot's living room. He sat next to a psychiatrist on the couch, underneath the print of children by a lake, declaring Dot incompetent, while a stenographer recorded the proceed-ings in shorthand. So Marcy gained control of Dot's finances, and Dot received disability checks until she was old enough for Social Security.

The money helped, but Marcy always felt guilty about her mother's indignity. Dot couldn't drive or vote, even if she'd wanted to, and her signature meant little.

Ten years before Dot died, my mother wrote to the lawyer who'd presided over the hearing, asking if there were any way to reverse the process. The lawyer — surely close to retirement— called my mother quickly. He remembered Dot well. "Ma'am," he said kindly, "your mother would have to pass a psychiatric exam. Do you really think that's possible?" My mom thanked him and hung up the phone.

Her Inspiring Romance with My Grandfather

Dot was married to Ralph for thirteen years. My other set of grandparents have been married for over sixty years; when I was little, my family visited them in a split-level we called "MaMa and Grandpa's." Granny and PaPa we visited separately, Granny in her house alone, PaPa with his sister Anita and his mother, Granny's "damn Pearl Carter," in their mustard-colored home on the other side of Huntington.

When I was very little, before PaPa died, I liked to imagine what he and Granny had been like as a couple. I knew they'd fought, she'd lied, and Ralph had screamed, angry and power-less, and finally Dot had locked him out. But I'd also heard my mother tell happier stories, how they'd smoked together on car trips with the windows rolled up.

Even now I like to imagine them: the workaholic railroad engineer with a wicked sense of humor, and Dot in her saner, more social days, when she and her pastor's wife went out to lunch. Ralph and Dot were a beautiful couple; perhaps that's why they got married. She was slim, black-haired, with a shy, bright smile and the deep tan complexion of her Cherokee mother. He had a boyish grin and dark brown wavy hair.

Once, on a visit to PaPa's, after he picked me up from kin-dergarten, I grew bored with the book I was reading, my lit-tle body stretched out across the thin brown rug. I looked up to where PaPa sat in his white leather chair, his prosthetic leg propped up alongside his real one as he drank a glass of iced tea-and-Tang and joked with Anita. I decided it was a good time to bring up Granny. I was curious to hear what he'd say, and I thought he'd like to hear how his ex-wife was doing. Perhaps, deep down, he loved her still.

I don't remember what I told him. Seconds into my story, the room shook with PaPa's laughter. "Granny!" he crowed, gripping the chair's armrests for support. "That's a *great* name for her." I stopped midsentence, confused and embarrassed, giggling as I pretended to understand the joke.

But the joke was on him, at least I thought so: I knew some-thing he didn't. Granny and PaPa owned matching recliners. Hers was pink and his blue. They seemed like "his and hers" models, like prizes they'd won together on a game show. I didn't think of the obvious, that there'd probably been a sale at the La-Z-Boy out-let, that my mom had helped purchase both chairs. When I visited Granny or PaPa, I sat in the recliners. I smiled to myself, thinking of their lifelong connection, about how love could not die.

When PaPa passed away, I told Granny all about it, though surely I knew she'd already heard. I wanted to see her reaction. "I feel like a weight has been lifted off my shoulders," she said, her tone low and solemn. She clutched a post on her porch and stared toward the floodwall. It seemed she was gazing through the concrete at the Guyandotte River. I was glad. To me this meant she still loved him. Her grieving over their lost romance had finally ended, and she felt relieved.

On the car ride home, I told my mother what Granny had said, and I was confused when she rolled her eyes and sighed. A few years later, I thought I finally understood: Granny had spoken out of spite. I realize now, after two decades of Granny's inconsistencies—sewing dresses for my sisters and me, giving us birthday money and then telling us to leave—that Granny's statement didn't necessarily mean she loved or hated PaPa. She might have just said it for dramatic effect.

Or maybe not. One winter day when my mother was at work in the blouse department, Dot appeared outside the store window, pacing the street. Marcy's supervisor gave her the rest of the day off, telling her to get her mother in out of the cold. As they rode the bus home, Dot explained. She'd walked out that morning, probably out of cigarettes, and she'd heard a voice tell her Ralph was at her house. "He's burned it to the ground, Marcy! We've got no place to go!" She rocked back and forth on the bus seat in terror. My mother hugged her, told her nothing had happened, but Dot would not be consoled. As the bus drew nearer to their street, Dot clenched my mother's hands. She bawled with relief when she saw the house was still there.

Her Tragic Fall and Rescue

On a July afternoon, two weeks before Granny died, her next-door neighbor, a woman in her seventies, called my mother, worried. Granny always picked up her paper at six a.m., and that day it lay lonely on the porch, its plastic wrapping limp in the heat. Knowing something must be wrong, my parents rushed over.

They pounded on the door, calling to Granny, but she didn't answer. They moved around the house, peering through the threadbare beige drapes that hung in her windows, banging on the glass, yelling, "Mother, it's us. Are you okay?" Still, the house stood silent, locked up tight. They considered the air conditioner, a gray metal box holding a window half-open, but it had taken both my dad and Uncle Bobby to install that heavy appliance earlier that summer. My parents decided to break down Granny's flimsy front door.

My dad stood on the porch, preparing to kick through the hollow wood with his black leather shoes, and another neighbor, a man in his thirties, noticed him from across the street. He and my dad removed Granny's air conditioner and set it on the lawn, and my mom climbed in through the window.

"Where are you, Mama?" my mother called as she searched the small house. "Are you hurt? We're here to help you."

At last she heard her mother's voice from the bathroom, a weak moan: "Go away."

My Family's Loving Eulogies

Before the service, I waited in the funeral home lounge with Uncle Bobby. I sat on the too-soft couch, my hands shaking, spilling tea from a Styrofoam cup onto my white skirt. Bobby walked in circles around the little room, his head bent, his bald crown looking bare without his usual ball cap. His own cup of tea rested on an antique end table, next to a blank sheet of notepaper.

Bobby intended to speak at Granny's funeral, but he hadn't yet decided what to say. Instead of jotting down thoughts about his mother, he told me stories of his solitary bike ride that summer through Yellowstone National Park. "I ran over the hill to pee, and I looked up, and there was a buffalo, that far away from me!" As Bobby pointed to the lounge wall to show the distance, a man in a stiff black suit cleared his throat. "The service is beginning," he said. The man directed Bobby to sit next to Lee and my parents in a wooden pew at the front of the chapel, and I sat next to my siblings at the back. Then Keith Leap began the sermon.

Reverend Leap had never met Dot. Faced with a sweet-looking elderly body in a casket he gave his one-size-fits-all grandmother sermon, clearly thinking it would apply to my Granny. But a one-size-fits-all T-shirt requires a head and arms to put through the holes. Some of Dot's missing appendages were a grandmother's patience, her resemblance to flowers, and the way she smiles down on the living from Above.

Sitting in the pew, I thought about Granny, remembering a conversation in her kitchen a year before. My mother had mentioned Granny's eventual "going to Glory" in an offhand, funny way. Granny had responded, hands on her hips, her grizzled eyebrows cocked, "What if I'm not going to Glory?" Leap closed his sermon with a call to repentance, instructing us to take inspiration from Dot's Christ-centered life.

Then Leap read a eulogy my mother had written about Dot's happier times: her work as a nurse, the birth of her children, her active devotion to the Methodist church. My mother cried silently in the pew as he read. We missed her, after all. I spoke next, willing my voice to be steady as I described her bright red nail polish, her love of fried chicken, and her room-sized collection of romance novels. I'd edited my speech several times, carefully deleting any allusion to mental illness.

"I feel like I'm really getting to know this dear sister," Leap said, smiling after I finished. Except for painting Dot a bit bland, his earlier remarks must have seemed appropriate to him. Then he asked if anyone else would like to share, and Bobby slowly rose from his seat.

As my uncle creaked up the steps to the pulpit, I wondered what he would say. He'd spoken at Pearl Carter's funeral, offering a few poetic lines about how his grandmother "thought of heaven often." Finally, Bobby stood alongside the pulpit. He closed his eyes for a moment before he spoke:

"For the last thirty years, my mother heard voices, and the voices were not kind."

Something Useful I Learned from Her as a Child

On Granny's rare visits to my house, she smoked outside on the concrete steps that led from the gravel driveway to our back door. When I was four, I sat next to her, my cheek against her polyester blouse, watching the pale gray smoke and the blue-tailed lizards that darted in and out of the cracks between the steps and the brick foundation. Despite Granny's fondness in her own house for smoking in the kitchen, drinking coffee at the table as the air grew thick and hazy, I believed she smoked outside at our house because she wanted to. I didn't know she'd been forbidden to smoke inside, that she sneaked and smoked in my parents' bed anyway when my dad was at work and my mom was cooking, that my mom wanted to keep Granny's fumes away from my dad's sensitive sinuses, my baby sister, and me. I thought Granny loved sitting under the sky, breathing in the scent of the mint and marigolds that grew around the steps, along with her nicotine.

"Come outside with me, honey, while I have a smoke," Granny said to me, as I sat among my dolls and picture books. She must have whispered so my mother wouldn't hear. I followed Granny, glad to be with her, and fascinated by her smoking.

I remember sitting by Granny in silence as ashes dropped into the mint leaves, our faces serious. When her cigarette burned down to a nub, she stubbed it out in the turquoise ceramic ashtray she carried in her purse. Then she stuck her tongue between her teeth, revealing a perfectly round indenta-tion where the end of the filter had pressed into her tongue. She took her thumb and forefinger and pulled on her tongue with her bright red fingernails, trying to straighten it out.

Later, alone, I pretended to smoke, puffing on twigs, raking my dull pink nails across my unmarked tongue.

Scissors

HILDHOOD PHOTOGRAPHS OF MY MOTHER show a skinny girl with freckles and an enormous bucktoothed grin. "Kids called me the human can opener," my mother says, shaking her head at her teeth in the pictures. I inherited her freckles and can-opener grin, and I'm grateful both of our mothers cared enough to pay for braces. My mother's head in her pictures is a mass of short, tight curls, often colorized dark red or blond, though her hair has always been brown.

The short curls were Dot's idea. Every few weeks, Dot marched little Marcy to a nearby basement where a woman sculpted her locks into a fresh pixie. When they got home, Dot sat her daughter down in a kitchen chair by the sink and whipped out a bag of narrow pink curlers. She administered a home permanent, frizzing and whorling Marcy's naturally curly hair. Years later, I witnessed this scene in reverse: Granny in the chair by the sink, my mother winding Granny's grizzled locks around the curlers. "Mind you make it even this time, honey," Granny said, patting her hair. "I don't want to look like a pincushion." A pungent cloud of permanent solution spread through the house, driving my siblings and me out onto the porch. I imagined my mother at my age, trapped in that chemical cloud, wishing to escape through a window.

My mother always hated getting a permanent, but I don't think she minded her short hair as a little girl. Marcy spent her afternoons bathing in creek mud or rescuing kittens; long hair would have gotten in her way. But as she got older, the other girls' hair grew long and straight, while hers stayed short and kinky. When Dot forgot to schedule a haircut, Marcy happily combed her few inches of hair, calculating the number of months that would pass before she could learn to French braid. But then Dot remembered. In tears, Marcy pleaded, but Dot had it cut anyway. Dot wanted her daughter's hair to mirror her own short, permed locks, and she wanted to stay in control.

Once, when Marcy was in junior high, Dot forgot about her daughter's hair for nearly a year. That was the year Dot locked Ralph out and Lee left for Vietnam. Before Lee shipped out, he came home for a visit. Marcy showed off her curls; they nearly reached her shoulders. Lee held his sister on his lap and brushed her hair.

"She'll be getting it cut tomorrow," Dot said when she saw them. Marcy trembled, picturing a middle-aged woman with a shiny pair of scissors and her locks on the beauty shop floor.

"Over my dead body," Lee snapped, standing up—his full five-foot-seven—and glowering. Lee was Dot's favorite child, and she listened when he spoke. My mother's hair has never been short since.

+ + +

IN the early mornings at Grace Christian School, the elementary students sat by class on the gym floor on bright strips of tape. The year I sat on the yellow line with the first graders, an eight-year-old brunette started a fad. One Monday, the girl burst through the gym door and sauntered toward the red line, tossing what was left of her hair. A fluffy mushroom stopped at her ears; the bottom half of her scalp was buzzed like a boy's. That haircut seems terribly ugly to me now, but it caught on.

Morning after morning, more little girls appeared on the lines with their heads part fluffy, part shaved.

I wanted that haircut. I didn't realize or care that my hair was dark blond, so the ultra-short part would look bald. Or that my hair was so thin the mushroom would look limp, as if it had been forgotten in the back of the refrigerator. One afternoon, I described the new hairstyle to my mother as she drove me home from school. "Wouldn't I look cute, Mommy?" I asked hopefully from the backseat.

To my shock, she dug her nails into the steering wheel, gritted her teeth at the rearview mirror, and growled her reply. "Okay, if that's what you want. We'll go to the beauty shop right now and get your hair *all cut off*. Is that what you want?"

"No, Mommy," I said, slinking lower in my booster seat. I'd stepped on a wound.

✦ ✦ ✦

As I grew older, I began to comprehend the damage those childhood haircuts must have done to my mother. Any movie with a pair of scissors upset her, and on-screen forced haircuts were as taboo as beheadings. Worst of all were film versions of *Jane Eyre*, in which an evil headmaster eradicates vanity in a school of orphan girls by snipping their hair to their scalps.

I respected my mother's feelings and kept my hair long, but I secretly wished it were short. All the popular girls had bobs. With our waist-length hair and Granny-made dresses, my sisters and I stood out even at our Fundamentalist Baptist school, where knee-length skirts and feminine hair were requirements for girls. "Is your family Mennonite? Or Pentecostal Holiness?" other kids asked me at recess. "No," I told them. "Just normal Pentecostal. We just like long hair." I felt nostalgic about pictures of myself at age four, when my hair had grown only a couple of inches past my chin.

In the eighth grade, at the height of my adolescent discontent, I nearly got my wish for short hair. One December morning, my mother was driving us to school, and a red pickup skidded into our lane on a patch of black ice. The truck struck us head on; the van spun around, and the truck slammed us again, crushing my passenger-side door. The impact broke seven of my bones and tangled my hair in the headrest. The emergency crew didn't have the patience to unravel the knotty mess piece by piece. "We're going to have to cut your hair to get you out, okay?" a man said. I nodded. My neck felt like the only part of me that could move.

Until that moment, my mother had seemed incapable of co-herent thought. She'd been asking me over and over in a high-pitched, nasal tone, "What happened? Did we have a wreck?" until I wanted to scream at her. But when the man pulled out a pair of scissors, my mother woke up. She shrieked, "Don't cut her hair!" The man didn't, and she went back to babbling.

When I felt well enough to go to church, I wrote an arti-cle about our car wreck for my youth group's newsletter. The climax of the piece was my miracle, when my mother woke up and saved my hair. I put *"Don't cut her hair!"* in italics. I couldn't tell the truth, that I'd been disappointed. If that paramedic had chopped off my hair, a friendly churchwoman might have taken me to a salon and let me pick out a haircut from the glossy stylebooks. Anything to make my hair look better while it was growing out.

My mother taped my article to the refrigerator in all its neon orange glory. She was proud of me for writing it, and she was proud of the story. I'd been hospitalized for five days. Every limb had a crack. My broken collarbones throbbed when I moved. Still, I got the feeling that if I'd climbed from the van, unscathed, with my hair cut off, my mother would have consid-ered it a greater misfortune.

✢   ✢   ✢

I'M getting close to thirty, and I have long hair, just like always. I'm not sure I'd recognize myself without it. When I get a trim, sometimes I ask the stylist to cut off an extra inch. I feel like I'm making a statement: I am an adult. I choose what to do with my hair. But I never seriously consider trimming more than a few inches; I fear the pain I'd see in my mother's eyes if I ever came home with it short. My hair is my mother's, not mine.

I have no idea how I'd look with short hair. I don't know if, given the choice, I'd wear it long. I prefer long-haired actresses. I feel a pang when girls get haircuts in movies, even if the long hair is a ratty wig. I compliment my girlfriends when they grow out their hair and hide a cringe when they cut it. I don't know if these feelings arise from my real taste or opinions, or if my mother is speaking through me. When I look at any woman's hair, I see the locks through my mother's eyes.

I don't think my mother knows she's being controlling. That she's walking backward in her mother's footsteps. I am glad she doesn't know this. By keeping my hair long, I'm joining my mother's team, standing against Dot's cruelty. When my mother sees hair between scissor blades, it's the 1960s, and she's sitting in a grimy salon chair. She looks down at the floor, already coated with frizzy curls, and she hears her mother's voice: *Take off the teensiest bit more.* My mother needs to spare her daughters that pain.

When I was little, my mother told me a story about Lee's daughter. Lee would never allow her to cut her hair, and when she turned eighteen, she came home with a pixie. Dot may have damaged Lee, too. "You see," my mother told me, "It's so important that you get to decide how you want to wear your hair. That's why I let you girls have your hair however you want." Of course, my mother wasn't telling us the truth, though I'm sure she meant to. The real tragedy of the story wasn't the control, but the haircut. She told my sisters and me we could cut our hair if we wanted to. Maybe that way we'd keep it long forever.

+ + +

Scissors

ONE of my sisters feels sad sometimes, and in the past, she turned her sadness against her hair. My mother has hurled the scissors into the ravine behind our house, to a place where only mice and snakes can find them.

Ten years after the car wreck, my sister found a pair of scissors on Thanksgiving morning. She cut part of her hair before anyone could stop her. Two swift snips in the front; she had to wear a toboggan when MaMa and Grandpa came over for dinner.

I think I understand why my sister did it. She was frustrated with my mother, seeking a way to rebel. My sisters and I love our mother, and our love shows us how to protect her sensitive feelings. We throw away wine when she visits, spare her the gritty details of our romantic disasters, recommend a new route if there's a dead cat by the main road. But our love also shows us how we could hurt her deeply. A stab in her gut: shacking up with a boyfriend, lighting a cigarette, having an abortion, cutting our hair. The haircut could be carried out alone, for free.

But my sister really wanted to punish herself, not my mother, and a haircut was a sure means of self-destruction. "We all have the face for long hair," my mother tells my sisters and me, though none of our faces are shaped the same. "We look so much prettier and younger with long hair." With a haircut, my sister attacked her own beauty.

Looking back, what strikes me most about the Thanksgiving haircut isn't the cut itself, but the way my mother reacted. My mother pulled into the driveway after a last-minute grocery run, and I raced outside, yelling, "She's got the scissors!"

A determined calm settled on my mother, the same calm that descended when an older boy accidentally ran over my six-year-old brother's leg with a bicycle, and bones angled through the skin. At the word "scissors," my mother left the car door open and strode purposefully through the back door, her brown curls flopping against her shoulders. "Where is she?"

my mother asked me, her voice collected and firm. This was a woman we could rally behind, a woman worth a few extra inches of hair.

My mother had no idea how much hair her daughter had cut off; there might have been nothing left. But she didn't have time for grief. She ran to her daughter, to stop her if she could. And if the worst had happened, she was ready to hold her and whisper that her hair would grow again.

Ghost Siblings

Christopher Michael

I have a brother. He is dead. My seven-year-old brother painstakingly penciled these words on a horizontally ruled sheet. In between each pair of solid lines on the page, a dashed line props up the middles of the trickier letters: the cross of the *t*, the *b*'s round belly. *I have three sisters,* Joshua began, before writing the sentences that must have made his first-grade teacher's tight perm stand on end.

A baby grew in my mother's left fallopian tube when I was eighteen months old, seven years before Joshua was born. When the tube burst, my mother plopped me into my crib and crawled to the bathtub, casting looks over her shoulder as I wailed. "That's the only time I ever let any of you cry!" she tells me, proud and apologetic. My mother stared at the cracked bathroom ceiling, hoping to soak away her stabs of pain. My dad wrapped his dripping young wife in a blanket and drove her to the hospital. The doctors were shocked she was alive.

Months later, when the baby should have been born, my mother grew depressed. She spent hours in her prayer closet, kneeling between a basket of baby clothes and her stained maternity dresses. Finally, revelation dawned. She'd tried to move on after her surgery, washing my cloth diapers and teaching Sunday school like nothing had happened, and she needed to mourn her child. To mourn properly, she needed the child's name.

My mother called her obstetrician, a kind middle-aged man, and asked if he knew the sex of her baby. "I'm sorry, Marcy," he told her, "but I just can't remember."

"Thank you so so much," my mom said, beaming into the receiver. The doctor couldn't *remember*. It *had* been possible to tell. She yanked her typewriter from its ponderous black case and banged out a letter to the hospital's records department. Then she raced down our gravel driveway toward the mailbox, ignoring the sharp rocks that bit into her bare feet.

Halfway to the mailbox, she stopped. She closed her eyes, face skyward, letting the wind rustle her cotton skirt and her long, curly brown hair. She ran back into the house, letter still in hand.

I don't remember this, of course, but she must have headed straight for my crib. My dad was at work, and I'm sure she needed to tell someone. "It's a boy," she breathed, gathering me up, warm and pink from my nap. Her tears dotted my undershirt. "God told me his name is Christopher Michael, and, my darling Sarah Beth, he looks a lot like you."

As I grew, my mother and I talked more about Christopher Michael, imagining the day we'd finally hug him in Heaven. My mother was a stay-at-home mom, and the daily absence of adult conversation gave her time for prayers and dreams. She taught me to make a prayer list: the U.S. president and our church pastor at the top, then parents, siblings, grandparents, great-aunts, regular aunts and uncles, cousins, my dog and pet snail, school friends, teachers, and classmates and teachers I hadn't forgiven. I penciled "Christopher Michael" into my list of siblings.

When I prayed for Christopher Michael, I pictured him running down the golden streets, a smaller, boy version of myself. Blue-green eyes. Too-skinny limbs. Stick-straight, honey-brown hair. A nose that should have been smaller. He probably didn't have my freckles, my dirt-brown host that budded in spring and blossomed after a day at the pool. That's one perk of a place that glows without sunshine: you can't get freckles from the Glory of God.

I prayed for Christopher Michael, but I didn't wish him into my life, crammed as it was with three mortal siblings. After Joshua was born, my dad converted our five-seater coupe into a six-seater sedan by buckling Jennifer and me into the front passenger seat. We had to share, even though we were the biggest; toddler Rebecca and newborn Joshua needed their safety seats. On the ride to church, the playground, my grandparents' house, Jennifer squashed against me in her sweaty T-shirt, surrounding me with her odors of wild onions and dogs.

"The seatbelt's too tight!" she screamed, without fail.

I adjusted the strap.

"Too loose!"

My mom joked that if Christopher Michael were in the car with us, she didn't know where we would put him. She said, "We'd have to strap him to the roof."

Christopher Michael wouldn't have fit any easier into our house, a 1,200-square-foot rancher with one bath and three small bedrooms. Rebecca's bedroom was filled with our toys and clothes, the bed Jennifer and I shared was crowded enough, and Joshua slept in a crib in the living room. Two beds by the piano would look ridiculous. And we couldn't handle another person in line for the toilet. When the family car pulled up in the driveway, my sisters and I yelled, "First on the potty!" The last girl to call dibs peed in the woods behind our house. My unborn brother was better off in his roomy mansion in Heaven.

I envied Christopher Michael his own gold-plated toilet, his cavernous playroom full of unimaginably exciting toys. I pictured his mansion as a fairytale castle with stone turrets, a coat of ivy, and red geraniums bursting from window boxes. When a Biblical celebrity strolled by, Christopher Michael hurried outside. "Moses, what does manna taste like? Did you see any interesting skeletons on the bottom of the Red Sea?" Christopher Michael could get immediate answers; I had to wait until Heaven to find out.

I envied my brother, but I pitied him, too. I kept his name on my rumpled prayer list because I worried he was lonely. Alone in his ruby-studded, race car-shaped bed, he might wish a dog-scented sibling was lying beside him.

Joy

Once a year, my mom drove to the other side of Huntington, West Virginia, toting a pitcher of water and a bouquet of roses. "We're going to see *my* sister," she said, smiling wistfully at me in the front seat, my sisters in the back. I hummed along to the hymns on the car radio, enjoying a seat to myself. My dad was at his parents' house with baby Joshua.

My mom turned at a man-made pond that was choked with water lilies and stopped under a shady tree. Then she unfastened Rebecca from her safety seat and handed me the pitcher. While my mom kept pace with Rebecca's short legs and Jennifer scampered off to catch cicadas, I sloshed ahead down a steep ridge until I came to a small, flat headstone. It was coated in mud from fresh graves. I poured the water—half on the grave, half on my socks—and my mom whipped a nylon brush from her purse and scrubbed until we could read the inscription. *Glenda Joyce Hager*, with birth and death dates less than a year apart.

Joy died six years before my mother was born. Dot got up in the night to smile into the crib, and her baby wasn't breathing. She rushed Joy to the hospital, but it was too late. A fast-killing case of meningitis. A couple of weeks earlier, Dot had dressed her baby in lace and stick-on hair bows for a batch of professional photos. Joy had whimpered, then giggled as the photographer danced a stuffed bear around the camera. On Dot's birthday, days after the funeral, the prints arrived in the mail.

I never heard Granny mention Joy, but my mother talked about her often. When I smacked Jennifer for knocking over my dollhouse, or whined when Rebecca used my new T-shirt as a nightgown, my mother got teary-eyed. "I would have given my right arm to have a sister," she told me. "You don't realize how blessed you are. I have to wait till Heaven to see mine."

My mom loves her two flesh-and-blood brothers. Lee danced with little Marcy to her favorite Elvis and country-western songs. One day, dressed in a white suit for the prom, Lee twirled his small, muddy sister around the front yard. I found her relationship with Bobby easier to understand. They'd left a permanent brown stain on their mother's ceiling by shaking a can of Coke until it exploded. Another time, Marcy fought Bobby for a box of Cheez-Its. They punched each other and tore at the box until crushed crackers coated the floor. But neither brother could replace a sister.

If Joy had lived, she might have played dolls with Marcy and tied ribbons in her hair. She might have helped her choose trendier skirts and blouses for high school, and taught her to twirl a baton well enough to make the majorette squad. She definitely wouldn't have joined the military at eighteen, like both of her brothers, and left Marcy alone. When Marcy grew up, Joy might have taken her out to lunch and chatted with her by the pool while their children swam.

Joy might have understood when Christopher Michael died, in a way that no one did. Years passed before my dad could comprehend how much the loss hurt Marcy. Her brothers didn't get it. Friends at her church were worst of all:

"It's just a miscarriage."

"The important thing is you're okay, honey."

"You're lucky you didn't lose a child you actually knew."

Christopher Michael(s)

I did miss Christopher Michael, at least for a while. I was lonely in high school, and I envied a blond brother-sister pair who were one grade apart, just like Christopher Michael and I might have been. When one of them dated, the boyfriend or girlfriend joined the siblings at their lunch table; when they were single, they prayed and ate happily, just the two of them. If Christopher Michael had lived, maybe I wouldn't have had to scramble for any empty foot of lunchroom bench, hoping someone would talk to me.

Joshua missed Christopher Michael, too, though he didn't long for him the way my mom longed for Joy, mourning the lost sibling of his own gender. His three older sisters picked up his toys, brought him Popsicles, let him ride the sled on the trek back up the snowy hill. As far as I can tell, Joshua mainly missed his brother when he wrote a play for us to perform. Jennifer could fake a man's voice decently, but Joshua tired of his ersatz male actor. Once, Jennifer giggled girlishly in the middle of a line, and Joshua threw the script in frustration. He screamed, "Christopher Michael would have done it better!"

And here lies the blessing and the problem: Christopher Michael is our design-your-own family member. I could conjure up a friend for the school lunchroom, and Joshua could add testosterone to his plays. A living Christopher Michael may have lacked the patience for living room theatricals and ignored his nerdy sister in public. I might have asked him to keep away. I could have eaten my school lunches with Jennifer, but I chose not to, and Marcy and Bobby didn't exist for each other within three blocks of school. But in an absence of sweating, opinionated proof, Christopher Michael could be whatever we needed.

Everyone in my family must expect a different Christopher Michael to greet us inside the pearly gates. Jennifer's Christopher Michael might have my small ears but larger eyes, and

Jennifer's own passion for roaming in the woods. Rebecca's might have my nose but higher cheekbones; he'd enjoy reality TV and picnics in the park. Joshua's Christopher Michael might share his gene for premature balding and his obsessive interest in obscure European bands. My dad never mentions his unearthly child, but I'd bet his version would fish for bluegill, catfish, and trout with more enthusiasm than his living kids can muster. My mom's version might be an athlete, to make up for her wimpy brood. We can shape Christopher Michael in our minds like a just-met potential lover, giving him traits that create the ideal companion for ourselves. And unlike the lover, he can't disappoint us by just being who he is, since we never see him at all.

Recently, I confessed these brotherly ruminations to a friend. I lowered my voice to a whisper, though my mother was two hundred miles away. "I'm afraid my mom will get to Heaven and look for Christopher Michael, and he'll be a *girl*."

My friend laughed. He's a man of faith, but not the kind to have a divine revelation on the way to the mailbox. "I think if your mother makes it that far—makes it to Heaven and finds her child—you don't have anything to worry about."

"You're right," I said, trying to laugh, too. I realized then how small my doubts were, but this logic couldn't quell my worries. I believe my mother's going to Heaven, and I believe in my mother, even if these two beliefs sometimes amount to the same thing. I'm not worried about my mother's faith. I worry my mother won't find the person she's expecting, and I fear the revelation will cause her pain.

Still, our Christopher Michael visions have their earthly consolations, and Earth is where we need the consoling. In Heaven, Marcy will have her mansion, her parents, her big sister—we at least know for certain that Joy is a girl. On Earth, Marcy's had the standard quiverful of terrestrial heartache. Her father had a heart attack, lost his leg, and died. Her mother went crazy, went blind, and died. Her parents got divorced, and her own marriage is sometimes rocky. She'd planned to go back to work when Joshua started kindergarten, but her poor health has trapped her at home. Aside from her husband and four living children, my mother doesn't have any close friends.

As for the earthbound children, we're all okay, but we're surrounded by earthly temptations. My mother agonizes over sex, porn, alcohol, weed, yoga, Harry Potter, high-caffeine espresso. It must comfort her to have one child safely across Heaven's finish line.

And so, I'll cherish my ghost brother, and I'll let him be whatever I wish for. When Joshua smokes Marlboro Reds then locks himself in his room, blasting music I can't stand, I can imagine up a brother I can talk to. My Christopher Michael mails me funny letters, rescues me when I drive into ditches, and laughs with me over *David Copperfield.*

And I imagine Joy as the friend my mother still needs. My mom sees her brothers at Christmas parties, at the bedsides of dying relatives, at unexpected graduations. They love each other but have little in common. But my Joy visits my mom every week to watch Fred Astaire tap-dance or Bing Crosby croon. After the movie, the women discuss Republican politics over herbal tea and trade recipes for potato soup and fudge.

Garbage-Bag Charity

RIVING HOME AFTER WITHDRAWING our Christmas money from the bank, my mother and I passed what looked like a teenage girl speed-walking down a street on the west side of Huntington, West Virginia. Her hair, blond with dark brown roots, hung to the waist of her white jacket—hood and hair flew out behind her hunched shoulders as she walked.

"Did you see that girl?" I asked my mom.

"Girl? You mean lady. She's got to be old as me. Or close, anyway."

We stopped at a traffic light next to a decaying warehouse, and I looked through our green minivan's salt-splattered back window and spotted the petite female powering past the McDonald's a couple of blocks behind us. From what I could tell, her face did look a little haggard for her clothing. She reminded me of a prostitute in tight flared jeans and a puffy nylon jacket my family had unsuccessfully offered a ride one night in a flea market parking lot.

My mom drove a few more blocks toward home before pulling over to the side of the road. We looked at each other. "Sarah Beth, we've got to go back. That woman looked like she might need help."

"Yes, I know."

We like to rescue people.

✦ ✦ ✦

MAYBE Marcy always loved to rescue people, but I think her urge got stronger in her midteens when she donned a heavy wooden cross necklace to proclaim her newfound faith, a symbol her drinking and smoking relatives openly mocked. "Oh, Lord," Aunt Anita said when she saw it. When Marcy chose her major at Marshall University, she found the one she thought would allow her to help people the most: social work.

In the late seventies and early eighties, Marcy drove up muddy back roads, paying calls on the needy inhabitants of the hollers of Wayne County, West Virginia. Alone, she visited old men guarding shacks with shotguns; bonnet-wearing women over a hundred years old hauling water from pumps; trailers so full of stray dogs that Marcy, then pregnant, had to run outside and vomit. She found herself spending more time fighting bureaucratic red tape than meeting the real needs she saw every day, and she became a reluctant specialist in forcing the unwanted elderly into nursing homes. The only tangible good she did was chatting with lonely old women, but she always had to move on to the next client before the women were ready to say good-bye. Marcy was only too glad to quit work when I was born and devote her life to raising me and the three others who followed.

But Marcy never quit helping people. Throughout my childhood, my mom boxed up tiny undershirts, dresses, sweaters, and short sets, passing on to relatives the clothes her latest baby had outgrown. When my mom had another baby, the relatives gave most of the clothes back and added a few of their own.

The clothes from relatives we were glad to get. We even expected them. The clothes were exchanged on a complete footing of equality. My mom considered helping out relatives more of a family duty than a charitable act, and when relatives gave her clothes in return, she felt thankful but not indebted. She knew the relatives felt the same way.

Altogether different were the clothes given to us at church. Perhaps our fellow church members felt the same Christian burning to help people that drove my mother into social work. But when they quenched it by giving black garbage bags of old clothes, even as a child I wondered if removing clutter from their houses was as strong a motivation as helping the deserving poor.

Though I feel it more strongly now than I could as a little girl, those clothes offended my family. We did not consider ourselves deserving poor, or poor at all. I can only assume my family was conspicuous to churchgoers with open hearts and overstuffed storage rooms because of the four children, a large number in our Pentecostal, birth-control-using congregation. We must have seemed likely candidates for a good, soul-satisfying rescue.

Without bothering to get to know us, our fellow church members assumed my parents could not afford to clothe their four young children. Overlooking the poorer church families, who included a small clan on welfare, these charitable souls considered my family needy, though we were always clean, always had something church-worthy to wear, and always had a vehicle and gas money to get us to church for all regular and special services. My dad had a good job at a pharmaceutical company; we weren't rich, but by no means did we need the cast-off clothes of strangers, offered like an expired bag of potato chips to a homeless person.

Years after the bags of clothes, Rebecca visited a friend's Nazarene church. "You've got four kids in your family?" exclaimed a middle-aged woman, narrowing her eyes at my sister. "Why, you don't look poor and dirty!" The number four still carried a stigma, but at least the woman actually looked at Rebecca. She did not look poor and dirty.

Multiple families at multiple churches blessed my family with giveaway bags. The process was nearly always the same. A woman who wouldn't talk to my family normally, perhaps the wife of a deacon or prominent local surgeon, approached my mother after the service. She poked her head into the nursery where my mother worked and we kids stayed after children's church let out. "I've got something for you, honey," the woman said. "Could you please move your car over to where I'm parked?"

After the last parents finished socializing and picked up their kids, we moved our car. Then we opened the trunk, an embarrassing step if the bags came during the years of our old Crown Victoria with flat blue paint. Originally equipped with the luxury function of a yellow button in the glove box that opened the trunk from the inside, the Crown Victoria's trunk had a broken latch and had to be lashed shut with red-and-black bungee cords.

The woman opened her trunk (with a key or a button on her keyless entry), and she or her husband took out several black garbage bags, stretched thin with clothing. She stowed them in our trunk on top of the striped beach towel the car's former owner had used to replace the original carpeting. Then she said something like, "There's all sizes. I'm sure most of it'll fit you or your girls, soon if not now, as fast as they're growing."

Unless I'm projecting my current feelings into the past, those bags insulted me as a little girl. However, like a Christmas present or a mystery-flavored sucker, the bags excited me, too. When we got home, I helped my mother drag the bags onto the deck. My sisters and I tore into the plastic, rifling the clothes that spilled over the wooden planks. With a few exceptions, the clothes were generally in bad shape: out of style, covered in fuzz, stained, and sometimes reeking of cigarette smoke. Still, every time someone gave us a fresh load of trash bags, I wondered what was inside. At the very least, I might get a new limp sundress for the collection I'd started in the back of my closet when I first found a purple and a yellow one in a giveaway bag. And, since we weren't rich, and there were four children to clothe, I hoped I'd find something I'd be proud to wear to church and school.

✢　✢　✢

THE road with the McDonald's was one way, so my mom turned down a one-lane brick street and circled the block to pass the woman again. We slowed when we spotted her, keeping pace with her rapid steps. "Roll down the window, Sarah Beth," my mom said. I had to yell a few times to get the woman's attention.

"Do you need a ride? We'd be happy to take you some-where," my mom called when the woman stopped and looked at us. Like the prostitute, the woman had heavy mascara and crow's feet around her watery blue eyes. Unlike the prostitute, she got into the minivan.

"Thank you. Bless you." She pointed a cold skinny finger down the street.

I reached behind the passenger seat to unlock the sliding door, and the woman got in, sitting behind me on the mid-dle bench seat. My mom started driving again, and the woman spoke after catching her breath. "I'm just heading to the apart-ments a few blocks from here, but I'm sure thankful to get out of the cold. Sorry I didn't notice you at first. I was so upset I couldn't see anything but the road ahead of me."

Of course, my mom had to ask why the woman was upset. And, like all the grocery store cashiers and obstetric nurses who had trusted my mother with their life stories less than a minute after meeting her, the woman told her. Her landlord, a man named Jake, had promised her extra time to come up with her three-hundred-dollar rent payment, but he hadn't put it in writing. Now he was demanding the money immediately. She was on her way to tell Jake she'd just taken on a second job at the little cigarette place up the road, so she'd have the money when she got paid the next week. The woman directed us as she talked, and we turned behind a used car lot and reached a crowd of green cinderblock buildings on an alley I'd never noticed before.

"Thank you so much. It's good to meet some nice people," the woman said, jumping out of the van.

"Wait a second," my mom called out, opening our white bank envelope, the one that bore the inscription "Season's Greetings" in red. She showed me the top inch of a twenty, raising her eyebrows in silent inquiry. Then she shook her head before putting it back and showing me a hundred-dollar bill. I hesitated—this represented a significant part of my siblings' and my Christmas presents—but then nodded *yes.*

My mom unbuckled her seatbelt and I cranked down the window on the passenger side. "Here. Please take this. Maybe it'll help tide you over," my mom said, leaning across me to stick the bill out the window.

The woman stared at the money for a moment, her eyes wide, then looked up at my mother. "Really? Are you sure?"

"Yes, please take it." The woman stood still for a second, then snatched the money as if it might melt into the snowy sludge at her feet.

"Then you've got to come in!" she cried. "Please! Just park anyplace. Right there in front of the building. You've got to meet my sister, or I know she'll never believe how I got this money. Nothing like this ever happened to us before. Angels! You've got to be angels."

+ + +

WE'D been angels before, though no one had ever called us that. For several years we'd felt like the divine-assigned guardians to one big, ever-growing family at our church.

This family, I'll call them the Smiths, lived on disability checks, pizza, and Mountain Dew. The Smith dad, Arthur, was thin and over six feet tall, all long legs and long arms. My dad called him "the man with the skinny head." The Smith mom, Lisa, was a small round woman, four feet tall with waist-length red hair. The first time I visited the Smiths' house, Arthur was letting his eight-month-old suckle at a Mountain Dew can. "My boy can't get enough liquid gold," he said. Arthur bowled in a local league in spite of his documented twisted spine. He was enterprising, though. He tried to increase the family income by selling drugs. He got caught and traded time in jail for employment as a nark. When we visited the Smiths, the stench of overflowing toilets, mildew, and rotting food hit me as one of the five tiny children opened the door in a diaper and stained T-shirt. I wondered if this was how the garbage-bag givers imagined our home life, "poor and dirty."

We'd met the Smith parents and brood in the church nursery, and this somehow led to a stream of urgent phone calls. We helped all we could. We brought diapers when they ran out and comforted Lisa and Arthur when a social worker took the kids away for a couple of months. We brought boxes of baby and toddler clothes, still in good shape after they'd been passed down through the four of us kids. To our knowledge, the Smith children never wore those clothes. We assume the shirts, skirts, pants, panties, and Underoos found new homes via a consignment shop.

We also brought Christmas presents so many years in a row that the Smith kids, and the parents, started treating us like Santa Claus, making requests. One Christmas, Arthur dropped a large box of toys toward my feet, catching it at the last moment as I handed it through the doorway. "Caught you not paying attention," he said. Arthur leaned his greasy bangs toward my forehead, his grin mischievous, childlike. I backed away quickly and stood in the driveway while my mother and sisters carried in the rest of the boxes. It was our last Christmas delivery. A few months later, the Smiths moved away to be close to Lisa's brother in Kentucky, and quit calling.

I admit I was glad to see them go. I think we all were, though my mom occasionally expressed a sincere, if unhopeful, wish that the family was doing well in their new home. They'd become a chore and seemed none the better long-term for our help. Although it is more blessed to give than to receive, a spontaneous act of charity brings the highest immediate blessing. The givers just have to believe the gift is doing the recipient good—they don't have to see it. In the Smiths' case, the giving became constant, a part-time job, and I started to wish for tangible results.

I at least expected some gratitude. Late in our relationship with the Smiths, Lisa gave us reason to believe that she, at least, was thankful. However, the entire family expected handouts like we had expected baby clothes from relatives, and the kids seemed to believe all good things came from charity. When my mother drove up in the Smiths' driveway in our new green minivan, after trading in the Crown Victoria with the bouncing trunk, one of the little girls put her hand on the bumper. "Who gave it to you?" she asked.

I'm not sure if other church members approached the Smiths after church and loaded trash bags of clothes into the trunk of their old used car. Maybe not. Giving clothes implied the recipients were worthy to wear what the giver had worn—to come after them, one firm step behind.

Maybe people did give the Smiths bags of clothes, but I know some members of our church didn't help them. When the Smiths' water got cut off, my mother called their deacon, the man responsible for the needs of church members in the Smiths' part of Huntington. His response was annoyance. He knew about that family, but didn't want to hear the next event in the sad saga of their lives. It was inconvenient in terms of time and expense, but my family headed to Walmart for water.

I can't remember, but I wouldn't be surprised if the deacon's wife was among the women who showed up at the nursery, offering us a trunk load of clothes. The charitable women probably did notice we didn't look poor and dirty. It was easy, comfortable, to give a bag of old clothes to a family who didn't need help and wouldn't ask for more.

+ + +

AT the blond woman's direction, my mom parked the van in what must have been the tenant parking lot. The pavement was cracked, with no painted lines or concrete markers, and, except for a small red sports car, it was empty. The woman noticed the sports car and said nervously, "Oh, good, Jake's here. I'll take you all upstairs, and you can be getting acquainted with my sister while I'm taking this money to my landlord." I looked again at the building's flaking paint, a tie-dyed bedsheet serving a first-story window as a curtain. I thought of the Smiths and wondered if I would need to hold my breath inside the apartment.

My mom and I followed the woman up a flight of narrow, concrete stairs built into a recess in the middle of the building, dark in the middle of the day from the cinder blocks that hemmed in both sides. "Sorry about all that trash," the woman said as I stepped over a molding pillow and half a dozen beer cans. "Our neighbors never pick up anything."

She opened the door at the top of the stairs. I didn't need to hold my breath. The apartment looked clean but brown. Brown paneled walls, thin brown carpeting, and two brown folding chairs lit by a small window and a bare lightbulb suspended from the ceiling.

"Jill! I had to bring these women up to meet you or you'd never believe it. Something wonderful has happened!" the woman cried. Another woman, thin as her sister, appeared from an adjoining room. I noticed her clothes before her face, tight jeans and a red, long-sleeved T-shirt marked with the logo of a brand I'd seen sold in the junior girls' department at JCPenney. When I looked up to answer her shy "hello," I was surprised at how young she looked. Her face was unlined, and her hair was long, light brown, and straight, like mine.

"This is Jill, and this is, oh I don't even know your names!" We introduced ourselves, and the blond woman told us her name was Claire.

"Jill, look what these people gave us!" Claire held up the hundred-dollar bill. "I just got me a new job down at that cigarette place a few blocks from here, and I was on my way to tell Jake, and—oh! I'd better go give him the money!" Claire opened the door and disappeared down the concrete hallway.

"Sit down if you want to," Jill said, waving a small hand toward the folding chairs. "I wish we had something better for you to sit on. We just moved in here last month, and at our last place they rented us furniture along with the apartment."

We insisted the chairs were fine and sat down. I wished almost immediately to stand back up because the way Jill stood, quietly staring at us in our chairs in that empty room, made me feel strangely royal. I was relieved when Claire returned.

"He took the money, and he's giving us three more days. We'll get it somehow," Claire said. She sighed, looking around the apartment like it was worth something, her face pink with happiness and cold.

"Here, you need to sit down more than I do," my mother said. She stood up, and I did, too.

"I never sit down. I walk everyplace, and I never sit down. People wonder how I keep so thin. It's because I'm always walking! Jill, I just had to bring them up here to meet you. They're angels!"

"We're not angels, believe me," my mother said, laughing. Jill smiled.

"Well," Claire said, uncertain. "Here's a picture of our daddy." She pointed to an unframed five-by-seven snapshot stuck to the paneled wall with a piece of Scotch tape.

"Oh," my mom said. "Does he live around here?" I walked over to study the photograph of the fat man in a chair with a black, pink, and green afghan tucked around his legs.

"He died," piped up Jill. I took a reverent step away from the picture.

"Yes," Claire said, giving the picture a loving pat. "We lost our daddy last year. While he was alive, we never needed anything."

"And our mother," Jill said.

"Yes," Claire said. "We had a beautiful mother. She died the year before our daddy died. I wish I had a picture here to show you. The girls miss their granny. She knew when we were having a hard time, and she'd send stuff to the girls—clothes, shoes, anything they needed."

"That sounds like my grandma," my mom said. "She did things like that, sent me boxes of clothes, and they were all in style. She knew my mother didn't have much money, and since she was an orphan, and a family adopted her to be their servant, she understood what it felt like to stick out from the other kids. Grandma was like another mother to me."

Claire and Jill smiled. "There's my girls' bedroom," Claire said. She looked at me and motioned toward the room where Jill was sitting when we arrived. "One's in high school, one's in middle school. My oldest is maybe about your age." Through the open door I could see two twin-size air mattresses on the floor, half covered by thin purple comforters. Magazine pictures of male heartthrobs coated the walls.

"You have a beautiful mother," Claire said to me, drawing her eyebrows together as if she were preaching a sermon. "I wish I'd put more value on my mother when I had her. You cherish that beautiful mother."

"Thanks," I said.

"Thank you," my mom said, rolling her eyes, but smiling, too.

+ + +

I do have a beautiful mother. I did back in the giveaway-bag years, too, even if the women at church often offered to arrange a free makeover. And the giveaway bags weren't just for us kids. They also included clothes for my mother. Most of the family clothing budget went to my siblings and me, so perhaps sometimes Marcy looked like she needed it.

Sometimes the bags were just for my mom, from people who didn't have kids, or kids at ages that made passing on clothes difficult. Once my mom wore a blouse to church she'd found in one of her exclusive bags. During the service, she saw the giver looking at the blouse from across the aisle, a satisfied smile on her face. My mom never wore it again. Or at least she never wore it again in public. Perhaps she gave the blouse to Goodwill, but it might have gone the way of a lot of the clothes in those give-away bags. We wore them when no one would see us.

The four of us kids came to depend on those clothes. We never had to buy clothes for hiking, sledding, or playing in the woods behind our house. For sledding, there was always a secondhand coat—perhaps hot pink from the last decade—no good for church or school, but great for soaking with melted snow and mud when we crashed into fences or unseen pits. For hiking, we had jeans, fuzzy flannel shirts, T-shirts from beaches we'd never visited. And, when we played, actors in unfilmed, unwatched movies, we had plenty of clothes to help us get into character: pioneers, farmers, rock stars.

So, perhaps we did appreciate the garbage-bag clothes. But we didn't do what I presume some of the givers imagined: hang their hand-me-downs with the best clothes in our closets, as treasures that would build our self-esteem.

+ + +

WHEN we left Claire and Jill's apartment and went home, my mom told the story to my dad, sisters, and brother. Then something struck her. Another way we could help. "Girls," she said, "I'm sure that woman's daughters need clothes. They can't have much. It broke my heart seeing how they were trying to make their room a home. Is there anything you can give them?"

I looked through my drawers and closet and found a few shirts and pairs of pants and jeans. The clothes were still nice, but a couple of years out of style. I'd already passed down most of the clothes I'd outgrown or no longer wore to my two sisters. Rebecca, who had no one to pass things down to, was able to give the most. My mom bagged up the clothes and drove them back to that small, bare apartment.

When my mom returned, she said, "Just that woman we picked up's sister was there, but she said she knows the girls will be excited to go through those bags." I pictured the girls opening the bags, as I had done before, hoping to find clothes that would make them feel a little better about themselves at school. I felt sick, wondering if I should have given some of the clothes I actually wore.

I wasn't the only one to have regrets. Years later, my mom still wonders if she did the right thing. Should she have paid Claire's rent, the whole three hundred? "But I couldn't. That money was for you kids. It didn't belong to me."

+ + +

ACCORDING to my mother, sometimes our acceptance of those bags was an act of kindness to the givers. We helped by transferring the clothes to the garbage can in the original black plastic. Sometimes the givers thanked us as they gave us the bags, happy the precious items they'd worn when they were young and thin or the outfits their children had outgrown would again see use. A sweater worn in a second-grade picture, that first basketball jersey, a T-shirt that came free with participation in a meaningful fund-raiser, a dress from dates with an eventual beloved husband, things the owners loved but no longer wanted to store, and in the eyes of anyone else had no business outside a landfill.

Some of our relatives have the same problem, giving us decades-old blouses, threadbare, yellowed, and frayed. "This has been in my closet for years just collecting dust," they'll say. "I'm so glad somebody's going to wear it again!" The relatives with the worst hoarding and donating problems are the oldest, the ones who lived through the Great Depression. MaMa gives me the belts she wore to church with Grandpa in the years after

World War II. She gloats when they won't reach around my waist. PaPa once lectured me as I sat on the toilet—a tiny girl—shaking the ceiling tiles with his voice because he caught me tearing off more than three squares of his one-ply toilet paper.

And PaPa hadn't gotten worse with age. When Marcy was little, Ralph had scavenged a rusted metal dollhouse with dog-chewed people from a neighbor's trash can in a nearby alley. He could have bought her a dollhouse easily, but in his mind it would have been a crime when there was one to be had for free next door. Ralph also scavenged in his own mother's trash can, rescuing a cracked glass punch bowl (useful as a dry decoration) and a miniature Nativity scene with chipped resin figurines.

Dot couldn't agree with Ralph enough to stay married to him, but they shared the Great Depression mind-set. Instead of throwing away the trashy knickknacks her ex-husband had brought into the house, as I imagine I would do, she kept and used them. Long after the divorce, the punchbowl graced Granny's coffee table, and she put out the Nativity scene every Christmas until she quit decorating a few years before she died. Like PaPa, she carried her cheapness into old age. After romance novels, Granny's favorite pastime during the twenty-five years I knew her was washing and hemming forty-year-old drapes. She hung some of them in her kitchen and offered the rest to my family as lavish gifts.

"Sometimes," my mom said once, "people need help throwing things away."

+ + +

WHEN Claire said good-bye that day, she promised to repay us as soon as she could. "It's a gift," my mom told her. "You don't pay back a gift." Claire seemed satisfied with that. She suspected she was entertaining angels, after all.

"I've got to thank you somehow, though," Claire said. "I know what I'll do. As soon as we've got the money I'm going to call and take you all out to dinner. You and all your girls." My mom told her it was unnecessary, but when Claire insisted, she asked Claire to promise not to think of it until she was so far ahead financially that there wasn't anything she could do for her family with that money. Claire agreed, but insisted she would definitely buy us a dinner. "You can write that down. You'll hear from me as soon as I can afford it. I'll never forget what you all did for me, my sister, and my girls."

Years have gone by, and she hasn't called. I hope she's forgotten, but I wonder if that family ever had enough extra money to buy restaurant food for helpful strangers. I think about Claire and Jill, maybe married, maybe still single, living together in a West Huntington apartment, pictures of the now grown girls taped to the paneled walls. I wonder about the girls, the oldest in her midtwenties by now. I wonder if they wanted to go to college, and if they were able. I wonder if they live with boyfriends or husbands in small brown apartments of their own, and if they'll end up with kids enough to attract a few garbage bags of clothes after Sunday service. I hope they're doing well.

I also wonder what happened to the Mountain Dew–drinking family, after they moved to Kentucky and didn't need us anymore or found someone else who could help. Unlike Claire, the Smiths didn't seem surprised by our assistance, though Lisa did wish to show my mother she was thankful. One year, a little before Christmas, when we visited the Smiths' house, Lisa reached to a high shelf in her living room and picked up a clear glass plate, holding it above her head out of reach of her children and several newly adopted stray dogs that were running circles around the living room.

"This is for you," Lisa said to my mom, handing her the plate. At first it looked to me like a dinner plate, then I noticed the etched winter scene and the words "Merry Christmas" above a year two Christmases past. Lisa had been to our house, seen my mother's collection of decorative plates on the walls.

My mom felt guilty about it, but she never put the gift up with her other plates, scenes of children from nursery rhymes.

While my mother was thanking Lisa for the plate, one of the little girls, a five-year-old with tangled blond curls, grabbed my hand and led me to the stairs. "Look," she said, pointing to a pile of dog shit.

"Why do poor families always think they need to help all the dogs?" my mom said on the drive home, which led into stories about the dogs she'd seen and smelled as a social worker. I wonder, too, why families like the Smiths with barely enough to care for themselves take in scruffy, homeless animals. People who could afford to care for stray dogs often ignore them or send them to the pound, considering them annoyances, as distasteful to deal with as the Smith family was to their deacon. Perhaps poor families take in dogs because they understand what it's like to be in need. Or maybe it's a way in their power of giving back, of answering their urge to give.

At His Feet as Dead

I WAS BAPTIZED IN THE HOLY SPIRIT WHEN I was ten years old. It happened in a Sunday school class at New Life Victory Center, a Pentecostal church in Huntington, West Virginia. The Sunday before, Ric, a pasty boy with twenty-five deadly allergies, had lain on the linoleum for most of the Bible lesson, apparently insensible to the world around him. My Sunday school teacher, Beryl, who wore baggy purple dresses and a helmet of gray curls, had fumed when two boys had picked up Ric's body and laid him out on the snack table. "Put him down!" she'd screamed. "Ric is in the throne room of Heaven, sitting at the feet of our Lord."

The throne room of Heaven! I imagined Ric, scrawny and freckled, sitting cross-legged on the gold pavement in front of two ten-foot-tall, marvelously handsome, bearded men. Father and Son slouched confidently on their marble thrones as the Holy Spirit flitted, ghost-like, behind them. The next Sunday, when Beryl asked if any of us wanted to receive the Spirit, I was first in line. I usually sat in the back, too shy to eat my stale graham crackers, but I wanted to see that throne room for myself.

I stood in front of Beryl, eyes half closed, thoughts focused on the Lord. I could smell musty perfume on Beryl's polyester dress, and I could feel both of her hands on my head, just above my ears. Ric, who already had the Holy Spirit, laid a palm on my arm. My friend Kati stood beside me in a cheap but clean floral dress, her hands cupped like she was catching rainwater. She rocked her heavy body back and forth. When the moment was right, Beryl pressed her fingers into my scalp and breathed, "Receive ye the Holy Ghost." Ric squeezed my arm. Both Beryl and Ric began to pray in tongues, a rhythmic cacophony of syllables. They waited for me to hear the *mighty rushing wind* of Pentecost, for my face to bloom with *cloven tongues like as of fire*. The air grew dense. I felt my white hair ribbon slide down the back of my neck.

I began to cry. I felt overwhelmed by the significance of the moment and afraid everything had gone wrong. I knew unfamiliar words — grammatically accurate sentences from a foreign language — were supposed to rise from my spirit, glorifying and petitioning the Heavenly Father in ways beyond my mortal understanding. My job was to speak the words aloud. But I didn't hear any words. Beryl and Ric prayed louder. I felt their breath on my face. A drop of Ric's sweat ran down my arm. Kati danced back and forth behind me, stretching her arms toward the ceiling.

Finally, I began, my voice small and tentative: *shenkava-donka.* I repeated a word my mother prayed as she drove me to school, putting the emphasis on *donk.* Every supernatural sentence she spoke seemed to begin with *shenkavadonka.* Occasionally, she gripped the steering wheel and plunged into a refrain: *don don don don don.*

Shenkavadonka, I whispered again, and then I launched into a flow of gibberish I hoped, wished, was genuine. "Praise the Lord!" Beryl cried. Satisfied, she transferred her hands to Kati's head and prayed in tongues again. Kati crashed to the ground like a lightning-struck oak; her head thumped the linoleum. Kati had entered the throne room, and I still waited outside.

But Ric wasn't satisfied. He was disappointed I still stood on my feet, that I hadn't been *slain in the Spirit.* I had not, like John in the book of Revelation, *fallen at His feet as dead.* Ric stepped in front of me with an attitude of authority, an attitude he might carry to the pulpit with him now, twenty years later, at the church he pastors in Haiti. He pressed his pasty forehead to mine and nearly shouted in tongues. He placed his hands on my head, and when I didn't fall, he tried to push me to the floor.

"No, Ric," said Beryl, spotting him just in time. "Let the Spirit do that. If she wants to go down, she'll go down."

At that point, my body felt weak, and it was a relief to sink to the floor. I dropped to my knees, put my arms behind me, and eased myself down. I gave my ruffled blue skirt a stealthy tug, making sure it covered my bottom. "Praise the Lord! She's received the baptism of the Holy Ghost!" Ric shouted. He moved back to Beryl's side, his smile beatific, smug. I hadn't dropped like a falling tree, but after I lay on the linoleum, no one could tell the difference. By this time, Beryl had made the rounds of the Sunday school room, and several more children lay on the floor. Along with Kati, I'd joined a girl in a lacy dress, a girl in a stained tank top, a girl in expensive jeans, and a boy in a wrinkled Oxford button-down. Perhaps the other children's spirits had journeyed to Jesus's feet, but mine had stayed in my body. The floor felt cold and dusty. I had graham cracker crumbs in my hair.

After a few minutes, a church elder walked by to say hello to Beryl, and he saw the little bodies on the floor. "What happened in here?" he asked, without alarm.

"We've had a move of the Spirit today," Beryl said with a proud sigh.

"That's wonderful," the elder said. He stepped into the room, his soles slapping inches from my head. I lay perfectly still, keeping my face free from expression. I wasn't sure if I was supposed to be able to hear.

✢ ✢ ✢

A few months before, after one of my family's first visits to New Life Victory Center, my dad had fumed during the long drive home. A deacon had sung "Holy Ghost Hop" as a solo during the Sunday evening service, and he'd literally hopped around the stage. "Rejoice. Rejoice. Rejoice! REJOICE!" He'd bounded higher on each *rejoice*, his tie and unbuttoned suit coat flapping around him. "I don't think I can handle it, Marcy," my dad said.

I giggled loudly in the dark backseat, hoping my laughter could keep the moment friendly. I would not say my parents had that terrible thing, a *bad marriage*, but they fought fairly often when I was little. Car fights were terrifying: my dad took winding, potholed roads at sixty miles an hour while my mom whimpered beside him. After my dad's complaint about "Holy Ghost Hop," I craned my neck to watch my mom in the rearview mirror. I feared she would light a fire by defending our new church. *Her* choice after years of dragging her children to whatever dry-as-dust Baptist church her husband had felt like attending that Sunday. Instead, she smiled and shook her head. "That man hopped. He really *hopped*," she said. My dad laughed, dissolving the tension, and I giggled again with relief.

I didn't realize my parents fought because marriage is hard, they were short on money, and they were very different people. When they got married, David took Marcy on his dream honeymoon: a damp, secluded cabin in the mountains of Beckley, West Virginia. All week, Marcy cooked in the cabin—eggs and bacon for breakfast, sandwiches for lunch, pots of spaghetti for dinner—and she sat on the muddy creek bank while her new husband tore worms in half and cast his line. "The most fun we had was pouring salt on slugs," my mother says now. She would have preferred a trip to a city, with pressed hotel sheets, lasagna baked by restaurant staff, and museums full of age-yellowed dresses.

My parents' religious differences were just one difference between them, a metaphor for their marital tension rather than the root cause. But I didn't understand this when I was ten. When my parents sat at the kitchen table, worn Bibles open, and spat darts about the baptism in the Holy Spirit, I believed if one of them would just accept the other's beliefs, they'd have no reason to fight.

So I lay on the Sunday school floor, pretending to utter words that flowed from my Spirit. The battle had been raging for long enough; I'd decided my mother was going to win.

✦ ✦ ✦

THE most visible differences between Pentecostals and Fundamentalist Baptists lay not in beliefs, but in religious expression. At Grace Gospel Church, my father's family's place of worship, a smiling old man in a black suit used his right arm as a director's stick, leading the four-hundred-member congregation through hymns in four-part harmony. Elderly women manned the piano and organ benches, their wobbling fingers supporting the melody.

"It is well!" the sopranos sang. They hit those three Gs with operatic gravity, hands clutching beat-up hymnbooks, eyes directed heavenward or at the director's bouncing hand. "It is well," the rest of the congregation rumbled in response. Two Es and a D for the clarinet-like altos; G, middle C, D for the trumpeting tenors; low C, E, G for the vocal tubas, the basses. Everyone knew their parts, by labor or by instinct, and everyone, it seemed, could read music. The sopranos raised their eyebrows and filled their chests, ready to hit those Gs again: "With my soul."

During the sermon at Grace Gospel, the congregation sat bolt upright, their mouths sealed shut. They smacked their children's legs when they wiggled. When the preacher made a better than usual point, one old man uttered a sonorous Amen. *The Amen Corner*, the other church members called him with a twinge of indulgence and embarrassment. The man had earned the right to speak since he'd been in the church for decades. And, as the church members grudgingly admitted, King David did say *Amen* in the Psalms.

On rare occasions, the pastor told a joke, and the congregation tittered politely. "You won't believe this, but I've heard some people who call themselves Christians suggest women should be deacons. Well, the Bible says right here that a deacon should be 'the husband of one wife.' Now, how many women do you know who are the husband of one wife?" A soft chorus of tittering.

At New Life Victory Center, the singing stars were the Praise Team, a group of snappily dressed middle-aged men and women who led the thousand-member congregation in contemporary songs that summoned the Spirit. "Shout to the Lord," "This is That, Spoken by the Prophet Joel," and my dad's dreaded "Holy Ghost Hop." A young woman in flashy makeup pounded a grand piano until it shook, and the Praise Band, men in khakis and loosened ties, banged drums and revved electric guitars. The congregation read lyrics—no music notes—from slips of paper found in the bulletin, leaving the harmonies to the Praise Team. The congregation needed their energy to dance.

During the praise and worship service, old and young raised their arms and shuffled back and forth. They stamped their feet, clapped wildly, and waved their arms in the air. They sobbed, shouted, twirled. They ran laps around the sanctuary, wearing lampshades they'd decorated with glitter pens. *Holy Ghost Party*, the lampshades read. *Drunk on Jesus. There's no high like the Most High.*

During the sermon, the congregation was all Amen Corner. It was Amen Corner gone wild. When Pastor Garrett, the preacher, made a good point, old and young jumped to their feet and shouted, and a man stood on his chair and prophesied in tongues. The congregation laughed in the Spirit for an hour at no joke at all, their guffaws contagious and uncontrollable.

Getting drunk. That's what we called this state of religious ecstasy, though drinking alcohol was a bitter sin. One Sunday evening, Pastor Garrett got so caught up in shouting he forgot to deliver his sermon. "Pastor was so drunk tonight," my mom said to a friend, her smile indulgent and knowing.

+ + +

TO someone unacquainted with these different styles of worship, Pentecostals and Fundamentalist Baptists must seem nearly identical: just two fiery branches of the Religious Right. Their tenets of belief are *almost* the same. Both groups believe Christ, the Son of God, was born of a virgin. Blood drawn by nails, a Roman soldier's spear, a crown of thorns, and a whip atoned for our sins. Christ emerged from His tomb, scarred but healthy, three days after His death, and He will return to earth on a cloud, trumpets sounding behind Him, to carry the faithful up to Heaven.

Both denominations believe water baptism of babies is an atrocity, since infants can't decide to follow the Lord. Both denominations evangelize rabidly, assaulting strangers with badly written tracts. Both denominations believe men bear a stronger resemblance to God's image than women, and they agree on the sorts of rascals who have boarded a bullet train to hell. Both denominations believe they aren't denominations at all, just believers who have found God's true path.

Both denominations are fundamentalist Christian, which means they believe every word of the Bible literally. The Israelites crossed the Red Sea on dry land, walking between walls of shining water. When Joshua needed more daylight to finish a battle, God reached down and held the sun still in the sky. Jesus fed five thousand people with the contents of a little boy's lunch pail. During the future Battle of Armageddon, blood will flow through the streets, deep enough to cover the horses' bridles. Every event in the Bible happened, or it will happen someday. God breathed through the pens of the Bible's writers, ensuring every word was true.

Now, when I tell friends about my background, I often lump my Fundamentalist Baptist and Pentecostal roots together and say I grew up fundamentalist Christian. For my Christian friends who know little of fundamentalism, the doctrinal differences between these two denominations seem minor, confusing, not worth mentioning. For my Buddhist friends, atheist friends, and Christian-harassed gay friends, there may be no difference between the denominations at all. But I can't see it this way. In my fundamentalist Christian circle, my Fundamentalist Baptist and Pentecostal parents seemed as far apart as Jews and Muslims, as the Yankees and the Red Sox, as Montagues and Capulets. Instead of taking the easy road of suicide, Romeo and Juliet had to live with being married.

I learned the most important doctrinal difference between Fundamentalist Baptists and Pentecostals as a little girl, from my parents' fights. My parents sat, facing each other, in the orange-and-brown kitchen chairs my mom's father had thrown out. They rested their balled fists on the wobbly beige table, and they held their legs askew to avoid the moldy tufts of padding that were bursting from the vinyl chairs' seams.

The language of the dispute came from the King James Version of the Bible, the most hallowed version for fundamentalist Christians of any variety. I grew up hearing the vocabulary and verb forms of 1611 mixed freely into Appalachian speech. *Diviner, aforetime, iniquity, idolatry. Spake, hast, blesseth, receiveth.* These words all sound normal to me.

The fights began when my dad got tired of my mom's radio preachers, when my mom got sick of her in-laws talking behind her back, when my mom and dad had to decide where we were going to church that Sunday.

When David and Marcy first got married, they'd compromised by attending a United Methodist church, the denomination Marcy had grown up in. Until I was three years old, I hung glittery, white decorations on the Chrismon tree, wriggled through the fifteen-minute sermons, and ate casseroles in a cold metal folding chair. Then Marcy started longing for a Pentecostal church, the faith she'd chosen at fifteen by listening to radio evangelists and reading *The Cross and the Switchblade* and *Set the Trumpet to Thy Mouth.* She wanted to go to Bethel Temple, a relatively quiet Pentecostal church decorated with Stars of David instead of crosses because the building used to be a synagogue. David tried it for a while, but the sermons annoyed him, and the forty-five minutes of singing hurt his back and legs. And New Life Victory Center was even worse.

Marcy felt she'd outgrown the Methodist church, so David decided to find a Baptist church she didn't hate. Our family visited every Baptist church in a thirty-mile radius. Grace Gospel Church, Rockwood Baptist, Souls for Christ, Church in the Valley. Wood pews, cloth pews. Choirs that stayed on key, choirs that wailed. Elderly preachers who snickered about praying in tongues. Young preachers who declared, "If one more person asks me about the Baptism in the Holy Spirit, I'll take out my sword and chop off his head."

For a couple of years, my parents found a church: Marcy loved a preacher from Georgia who pastored First Baptist Church of Ceredo, a congregation four miles from our house. He respected Christians of different denominations, and he had a charming Australian accent he'd picked up during his missionary work. Before the Wednesday night service, we ate spaghetti in the church basement, and during Sunday school, I played on the church's fancy playground. Then the preacher moved to a church in another state, and my parents' fights began again.

At the kitchen table, my dad opened his heavy brown Bible to First Corinthians chapter 13 and tapped verse 8 with his index finger. "'Whether there be tongues, they shall cease.'

See, Marcy? Tongues shall cease! They've *ceased*, Marcy. They're done with."

"Well, David, that verse also says knowledge is going to 'vanish away.' Let me know when that has happened, and I'll listen to your 'tongues shall cease' crap." The argument paused as my mom grabbed my whimpering baby sister from the living room crib and started breastfeeding her under a cotton blanket. "And if you'll look just a little further down the page to chapter 14, you'll see God's instructions for praying in tongues in the church. We're supposed to throw out that whole chapter, are we?"

My dad ignored her question and tried another approach. "The baptism in the Holy Spirit—it's just salvation, Marcy. They're the same thing. The Holy Spirit comes in and starts convicting you when you're sinning, the minute you pray the sinner's prayer." My dad tried to sound patient, but his voice was condescending and weary. He rumpled his thinning hair and covered his face with his hands.

My mom sat up straight, baby and all, hazel eyes flashing with anger. She used her free hand to toss her long curly hair. "I know the Holy Spirit convicts believers, David. Don't get high and mighty on me. What I'm talking about is the baptism in the Holy Spirit. You Baptists like to forget about Acts 19:2, when Paul asks that group of new believers, 'Have ye received the Holy Ghost SINCE YE BELIEVED?'" She grabbed the Bible and flipped sixty tissue-thin pages. "Look, David, there it is."

My dad, like any good Fundamentalist Baptist, was offended by the idea that the great miracle of salvation—"If any man be in Christ, he is a new creature"; "For by grace are ye saved through faith"—could be in any way faulty, incomplete. He believed the Spirit entered a believer as part of salvation, ready to sweep out the cobwebs of sin. My mother also believed the Spirit swept out new believers, but she didn't believe new believers were *filled* with the Spirit, possessing the maximum level of wisdom and guidance from the Lord. To be filled with the Spirit, a believer needed a second experience. She needed to speak in tongues.

Eventually, my parents abandoned Biblical logic and sunk into arguments of emotion. "I don't want the children to grow up confused, Marcy," my dad said, and my mom started to cry.

But after my experience on the Sunday school floor, my mom held a trump card. "The children aren't confused, David," she responded, her eyes triumphant. "They're choosing to follow the truth."

✢   ✢   ✢

FOR years, it didn't matter that I'd faked my spiritual baptism. On the car ride home from church that Sunday, I declared to my parents I'd received the Holy Ghost and spoken in tongues. Already, I felt only a twinge of remorse over my falsehood, even if I did stare at the dog hair on the car floor instead of the disappointment and glee on my parents' faces. My baptism served as my initiation into the Pentecostal faith, and my commitment, at least, was real. I'd left my Fundamentalist Baptist and Methodist roots behind me, and I had become a Pentecostal.

After that day, I cupped my hands upward like Kati when I prayed and sang in the sanctuary or Sunday school. I was too shy to dance, run laps, or don a decorated lampshade, but I managed to sway back and forth between my mother, who danced, arms stretched toward the ceiling, and my father, who kept both feet on the floor and his arms stiff at his sides. I prayed in tongues under my breath; I always began with *shenkavadonka* and tried not to think about the rest. After all, the words were supposed to come from my spirit, not my mind.

I'm sure my decision to become Pentecostal affected my parents' decision to stay at New Life Victory Center. My mother and I were happy, and we outnumbered my unhappy dad. My mother became the spiritual leader of the home, something unusual and progressive for a Fundamentalist Baptist or a Pentecostal family, where the husband leads and the wife submits. My dad's Baptist faith went from a dominant force in our home to something inferior and othered. I laughed without thinking at Pastor Garrett's Biblical jokes about Baptists. "Those uptight people are 'having a form of godliness but denying the power thereof. From such turn a-WAY!'" In a sanctuary full of dancing, hollering, prophesying Pentecostals, my silent father stuck out.

I should have felt more sympathy for my father. I understood what it was like to feel ostracized. My parents had enrolled me in Grace Christian School when I was five, back in their Baptist church phase, and they kept me there through the twelfth grade, years after our family was firmly Pentecostal. At my Fundamentalist Baptist school, attending New Life Victory Center promoted me from bookish, uncoordinated nerd to an outcast. It was quietly understood that I'd never have a date to the fall or spring formals, and I felt physically ill before lunch and daily chapel, worrying about where I would sit. Ironically, I faced this intolerance because I attended a Christian school. At a public school, I would have just been a generic "Christian," and Wayne County, West Virginia, is loaded with Christians. But at a school where Bible is an academic subject, every minuscule doctrinal difference was magnified.

As I got older, I realized that at Grace Christian School, the only Christians more lowly than Pentecostals were Catholics, since Catholics practiced idolatry and drank. According to my Bible teacher, God did allow a few Catholics into Heaven in spite of their Catholicism, but most of them were riding the bullet train to hell. To speed to hell faster, a person needed to ascribe to another religion entirely, like Buddhism or Islam, or one of those so-called "Christian" cults whose members show up in twos at your door. By contrast, Pentecostals were *possibly* headed to Heaven, but they needed to learn plenty about God's Word.

In junior high and high school, teachers cornered me in hallways and stairwells. They asked me, "Is it true that you handle snakes at your church?" No, I did not handle snakes. Other times, they offered me special privileges because of my misfortune, their voices dripping with sympathy. "I've heard your church doesn't get out until midnight. Don't worry if you need extra time on your homework." Sometimes Pastor Garrett laughed in the Spirit until one in the morning, but I didn't need their extra time. Once, on a field trip, a young, male teacher placed his hand on my forehead. "May you be healed, my child!" he bellowed, imitating Pentecostal televangelists, and my classmates smirked and laughed. I was too embarrassed to notice he'd stuck a banana sticker on my forehead.

The students were even worse. They'd been trained and guilted into constant witnessing, and they were itching for someone to witness to. Our school was virtually free from hardened sinners, so Pentecostals were an easy target. Often, when we had a few minutes of quiet work time, students surrounded my desk in their private school skirts and khakis, voices and index fingers raised. A student with homemade polyester knit pants and a thick mat of brown hair asked the teacher if he could run to his locker for his Bible, saying he needed to "show something to Sarah Beth." Most students ignored this boy on ordinary occasions, but he was a leader in moments like these. The teacher always let him go to his locker. I was by far the best student in my class, and the teachers were embarrassed I was so doctrinally screwed up.

Bible in hand, the boy in the knit pants flipped to his favorite passages and waved the red letters in my face like a loaded pistol. The other students crowded around me and repeated whatever the boy said. I could smell their hairspray, cologne, and sweat. No one listened when I argued, so I tried to imagine the students away and focus on my trigonometry problems.

In this hostile environment, I managed to fall in love, though there was never a chance he'd love me back. There were boys of more tolerant denominations available—Methodists, Presbyterians—but I chose a Fundamentalist Baptist named Nick Joyce. I loved him for his doodles in his textbooks, his three-point shot, his Christian rock band that defied the school's rules, his interest in angels and the trinity. "God's three different people, but there's just one God," he'd say, flashing his crooked smile at the girls around him. "I can almost understand it for a second, and then my brain freezes up." I sighed with longing every time he said this.

Oddly enough, Nick fell in love with Sherri, the only other Pentecostal member of our class. The Baptist kids gossiped about her beliefs, but they didn't ostracize her like me, probably because she was so much more fun. Sherri could staple her skirt into pants and do headstands during study hall, and she could perform back flips without touching the floor. During the year Nick and Sherri dated, Nick brought his Bible to lunch, hoping to work out their theological differences.

Nick planted the book's leather cover in a pile of sandwich crumbs and read verses between sips of Mr. Pibb. Sherri had no interest in fighting about the Bible; she chewed her pizza or talked to someone else. "We have to figure this out, Sherri," he pleaded. "We have to decide what we're going to teach our children!" I understood the gravity of Nick's lament.

I wonder now if I loved Nick because I wanted to replicate my parents' marriage, to seek comfort in a known form of misery.

+ + +

I was slain in the Spirit when I was thirteen years old, in an experience I believe was real.

Every Sunday after praise and worship, Pastor Garrett descended the steps from the pulpit platform to the sanctuary floor, and he stood in the broad space that served as the altar.

New Life Victory Center had a larger gap between the platform and the front row of worshippers than Grace Gospel Church. The altar at Grace Gospel was designed for the kneeling penitent; New Life needed space for bodies on the floor.

The morning of my experience, Pastor Garrett prayed in tongues and stretched his fingers while a deacon spoke into the microphone. "Please come forward if you're in need of prayer, and Pastor will lay hands on you. You've got to bring your faith with you! Remember when the woman with the issue of blood touched the hem of Jesus's garment? He said, 'Daughter, your FAITH has made you whole.'" And the people flooded forward: cancerous, lustful, overweight, barren, bankrupt, discouraged. My stomach dropped as the petitioners lined up. I felt I was meant to be one of them. After a glance at my dancing mother and silent father, I took a few slow steps, then jogged from our seats at the back of the sanctuary up to the end of the line. If I didn't move quickly, I was afraid I'd lose my courage and miss out on something momentous.

I went forward because I wanted to flood myself with the Spirit. But I also went because I was obsessed with the spectacle. When my dad stayed home from church, my mom and I sat on the front row. We loved to watch the line of believers falling under Pastor Garrett's hand. That hand seemed to wield the power Jesus had used to cleanse lepers, to raise Lazarus from the dead, to calm the winds and the sea.

The deacon lined up the first set of petitioners across the front of the church, and Pastor Garrett began at the far right. A willowy woman stood at the pastor's side, her left arm laden with satin cloths, dyed mauve to match the carpet. Two brawny ushers in maroon suit coats stood behind a tiny elderly woman, their knees bent, arms outstretched. The pastor closed his eyes for a few moments, his lips trembling with tongues. Then he pressed his hand into the woman's gray perm, and she dropped instantly into the ushers' arms. The ushers eased her onto the carpet, and the willowy woman covered her legs with a cloth. Then Pastor Garrett, the ushers, and the cloth-draping woman moved on to the next petitioner.

About twenty people separated me from the power in the pastor's hand. A middle-aged woman waited in front of me, dancing in scuffed high heels. A man with a suit and ponytail waited quietly behind me, one dignified hand toward the sky. I wadded the sweaty sides of my flower-print church dress, trying to keep myself from shaking.

The line moved slowly, since we had to wait for the petitioners to leave the throne room of God. When someone straightened her skirt and got up, a deacon hurried another person to the front, placing her in front of the empty spot on the floor. Eventually, I got close enough to watch the people on the carpet. Old men in plaid pants and polyester support socks, middle-aged women in blouses and jumpers, young women in tank tops, teenage boys in jeans. Some lay like peaceful corpses, spirits voyaging, and some raised their arms and prayed in tongues aloud. They prolonged the experience as long as they could; standing up took more faith than falling. When the petitioners stood up and walked back to their seats, they hoped to discover they were healed.

Sometimes, before Pastor Garrett laid hands on a petitioner, he spoke with the person for a few moments, then he took the microphone and told the church what the person was praying for. A short woman with bad teeth and old clothes had gotten her fallopian tubes cut, tied, and burnt during a bad marriage, and now she wanted to have a baby. A tall man with spiked, electric-blond hair and leather pants asked to be cured of AIDS. He claimed he'd "repented from his homosexual sins." A few years later, the woman with bad teeth gave birth to a healthy girl she named Faith. The man with the leather pants disappeared from the church.

Finally, the deacon moved me to an empty space, next to the elderly woman who'd been first in line and still lay on the carpet. I was close enough to see Pastor Garrett's silver mustache, the hair follicles on his large chin, the thin white stripes on his gray suit, the glint of his black shoes under the fluorescent lighting. I could hear the tongues he prayed softly to himself, and I still remember one word: *shonda.* The pastor laid his hand on the forehead of the woman in scuffed high heels. She let out a shout and dropped into the ushers' arms. Then Pastor Garrett stepped in front of me.

Pastor Garrett didn't ask me why I needed prayer. That's probably why I don't remember the reason. If he'd asked, I likely would have said, "Boldness to share God's Word," and silently I would have prayed for one of my daily requests: a date with Nick Joyce, a pair of Adidas running shoes to replace my embarrassing high-tops from Walmart, a new friend who would sit with me at school. But all of these petitions fled from my mind when I felt the pastor's large, warm hand on my forehead.

When the hand touched me, a hundred-pound weight seemed to press down on my body. My knees buckled, and I had no choice but to fall to the floor. I opened my eyes right away, and I fingered the mauve cloth across my legs with a mixture of pride and embarrassment. I closed my eyes and breathed deeply: the air on the floor felt sweet and cool, the air above me noxious and hot. I wasn't sure how long I should lie there. My body felt small next to the man with the suit and ponytail, now stretched out beside me on the carpet. After a couple of minutes, I began to feel silly, so I got up and shuffled to my seat. Back in the congregation, I closed my eyes and raised my hands higher than ever, believing I'd earned a special connection with the Lord.

On the car ride home, I kept up a constant chatter to my siblings, asking them about their Sunday school crafts and the Kool-Aid stains on their dresses. I knew I had offended my father with my blatant display of Pentecostalism. My spiritual baptism had created a distance between us, but we were still fairly close. On car rides, he joked and caught my eye in the rearview mirror; that day he kept his eyes on the road. "I'm so proud of you for going forward, Sarah Beth," my mother said. My dad tightened his jaw.

My dad punished me for going forward a few days later, after I'd forgotten to expect it. Jennifer annoyed me, and I smacked her hard on the top of her head. Too late, I noticed my dad watching from the doorway, so I started walking toward my room. I wondered if I wouldn't be allowed to read for a month, or he'd give me a spanking. Instead, my dad merely spoke. "Why don't you get the preacher to lay hands on you so you'll quit hitting your sister?" I walked faster so I could cry into my pillow.

✛ ✛ ✛

MY dad was baptized in the Holy Spirit at forty-three years old, on the cardiac stepdown floor of Cabell Huntington Hospital. It happened six years after my spiritual baptism, three years after I was slain in the Spirit.

David was playing Frisbee with his brothers after a Fourth of July picnic, and suddenly he couldn't catch his breath. In pictures from that day, David looks unusually flabby in his T-shirt and swim trunks, and his face looks droopy and pale. He tried to claim he'd be okay if he sat on the grass for a minute, but he had trouble getting out the words. His older brother drove him to the hospital.

The doctors put David on the floor with the heart patients, telling him he was experiencing symptoms of a heart attack. They glued monitors to his chest and made him run on a treadmill until he feared he'd enter God's throne room for good. From his bed, he could hear a chorus of beeping heartbeats; every few minutes, a heartbeat settled into a monotone whine and set off an alarm. Over the intercom,

David heard a nurse yell "Code Blue!" and then he heard the jolt of the paddles.

During those nights on the heart floor, David needed comfort, and he found himself praying aloud. He closed his eyes and put his needle-pricked hands in the air, and suddenly he was speaking in tongues.

I visited my dad in the hospital after his spiritual baptism. My mother sat on his bed, cradling his left arm, her tears spotting her husband's nightgown. "Girls," my mother kept repeating, "your daddy spoke in tongues." My dad grabbed my arm and held it tight. All he said was, "Hi, Sarah Beth." Because I was sixteen years old, I mainly felt embarrassed, but underneath my teenage temper, I felt something stir. The arm grasp and the way my dad said my name felt like a plea for peace, an apology. An apology for his nastiness after I was slain in the Spirit, for all those Baptist churches, for dividing the family for so long. For the secret belief he'd held since the day he'd gotten married: "I'll get those tongues out of Marcy because they're not real in the first place."

A week later, David left the hospital twenty pounds lighter. What was left of him was filled with the Spirit. He had a lightness in his face and his step, as if he'd left part of himself behind with his weight.

The next Sunday morning, my mom and I were scheduled to work in the church nursery, and as a rule, my dad skipped church when he had to sit by himself. That morning, my dad sat alone, he raised a shy hand during the singing, and he went forward when Pastor Garrett offered prayer. When the pastor made it down the line to David, my dad said he wanted to testify, and the pastor handed him the microphone. David said, "There I was in the hospital, Code Blues going off all around me, and suddenly I had my hand in the air and I was praying in tongues!" After church, I listened to my dad's testimony on the cassette tape of the service, and I could hear the congregation's shouts and laughter.

My dad's spiritual baptism didn't fix my parents' marriage. My dad still spent plenty of nights on the futon, and we kids still tensed every muscle for weeks until our parents spoke, and we could breathe again. But life in the Childers household improved.

My dad quit complaining about the doctrines and riotous behavior at New Life Victory Center. He raised his right hand during the praying and singing, so he quit attracting embarrassing stares. He didn't get angry when I went forward in church. When kids at school asked me about my family's denomination, I could reply "Pentecostal," my eyes flashing with defiance, without feeling I was lying about my father.

And after that trip to the hospital, David started treating Marcy with more respect. This change might have come from the Spirit or his near-death experience, or a combination of the two. In any case, he was no longer the man who'd drag his wife to a cabin without discussion. In the Fundamentalist Baptist church, he'd grown up on sermons of "Wives, submit yourselves unto your own husbands, as unto the Lord," and he'd believed God had wanted him to be the family's dictator. After that trip to the hospital, my parents made decisions together. Often, he submitted unto her.

A few years later, David submitted unto Marcy when she decided to leave New Life Victory Center. As the church had grown, Pastor Garrett's attitude had changed, and my mother was fed up with the church's belittling of women and the pastor's sermons about pastoral authority. "You must respect and obey your pastor," Pastor Garrett said, too stern to laugh in the Spirit. "The Israelites respected and obeyed Moses and Joshua, and the disciples respected and obeyed Jesus. You should be the same way with me." My mother could handle only so much of this. For several years, my family visited every Pentecostal church in the area, in a reprise of our Baptist church tour years before. Churches like New Life Victory Center in expensive buildings, churches in high schools shut down for asbestos, churches in strip malls, churches in civic centers, churches on basketball courts.

Finally, my mother decided against all of these churches. For the last ten years, my family and several of our dogs and cats have gathered in the living room for half an hour on Sunday mornings. Our pews are the couch and the La-Z-Boy. "It's time for service!" my mother calls, dragging her husband and children away from the TV or out of bed. When I'm miles from home, as I usually am these days, I join the family service via speakerphone. My mother reads a few verses, someone takes a dog out to pee, then she reads a few verses more. At the end, she prays over our worries for the week. If she's lucky, we've all stayed awake.

+ + +

NEARLY two decades have passed since my spiritual baptism, and it matters now that my experience was faked. I don't regret my decision to join my mother's faith, but my lie makes me feel less a part of it. I've prayed in tongues many times in my life, and I believe every word has been a fraud.

I know I'm not the only one. I have a close friend, Hannah, who grew up in a Pentecostal church in Maryland. Her tongues began with *de la la*, a phrase she invented, thinking it sounded holy. Each word held a higher pitch, like three notes in a musical scale. Hannah raised her hands and weaved back and forth, then she murmured or yelled her sacred words.

After my dad got baptized in the Holy Spirit, he spoke to my sister Rebecca about praying in tongues. She was only ten, but she'd been baptized in the Holy Spirit for several years, and my dad wanted her to help him understand it. He asked her, "What does it sound like when you pray in tongues?" Rebecca blushed to reveal something so private. Then she told him: *leg-a-lamb*. It took my dad several minutes to stop laughing. My sister had never eaten leg of lamb, and she didn't realize she'd heard the phrase before.

Pentecostal preachers like to advise the faithful to "start out in the flesh, and you'll end up in the Spirit." My mother has often said the same thing, when she issues her commands for me to "pray in the Spirit every day!" across the dinner table, over the phone, in her e-mails. In essence, the preachers mean you should start out with gibberish, and the words that follow will be real. I'm unable to accept this. I feel that speaking gibberish even for a moment is a mockery of the Spirit. A mockery of people who believe tongues are real. *Shenkava-donka. De la la. Leg-a-lamb.* I can't believe these words bring us closer to God.

I believe my mother is sincere in her own tongues, and I'm sure many Pentecostals are sincere. My mother used her tongues to give birth twice without painkillers. Years later, she prayed in tongues during a complicated hysterectomy; she'd agreed to only a local anesthetic, trusting prayers over general anesthesia. I have no problem believing my mother is praying in the Spirit, even if her sentences still begin with *shenkavadonka*. But I know I was never sincere.

It bothers me that I lied for so long, so often my lies became unconscious, and I could fake my prayers without feeling any guilt. It bothers me especially now that I haven't been to church in ten years, beyond the prayer group in my parents' living room. It would be all the easier to deny my Pentecostal roots, since my commitment was rooted in a lie. And if I give up on the tongues, might everything else fall away? The Red Sea crossing, Armageddon, the little boy's lunch pail.

A couple of years ago, I talked to my friend Patrick about this crisis of faith, outside on a snowy night in upstate New York. He was drunk, *real* drunk, not drunk on the Spirit. I tried to tug him by his coat toward the road where he lived, but he kept stopping to admire the miracles of nature.

"Look at that tree!" he cried, his Irish accent thickened with alcohol. He took off his hat and let the snow fall on his bald head. "Look at that beautiful tree!" He'd paused in front of a snow-covered pine in the city park, one of many that looked just the same.

"That's amazing," I said. I focused as earnestly as I could on the tree's branches, needles, and trunk, illuminated by a streetlamp.

The moment felt strangely like a spiritual epiphany, so I told Patrick my worries. The tongues. The spiritual baptism. Getting slain in the Spirit. As an educated woman who tried to love people of all backgrounds, all faiths, I feared these beliefs were silly, embarrassing, and legitimately offensive to some people. And I feared I held these beliefs only because I loved my mother.

"But if you don't believe that stuff, what's left?" Patrick asked me, kicking his boot through a pile of snow. "Just the fucking boring, useless parts of your religion. You know something?" He lowered his voice so the tree couldn't hear us. "I still pray my rosary at night. Especially when I'm stressed. You know, I do."

Patrick grew up in a strict Catholic home in rural Ireland, and the strict Catholicism was a reason he'd left home at sixteen. But he couldn't run away from his faith. He told me he had friends who had remained Catholic for the tradition and community, but they were too intellectual for the supernatural elements. The Virgin Birth, Christ's resurrection, the saints who pray at the foot of God's throne, the pools of water that heal the sick, the transformation of bread into crucified flesh.

"But what's the point of that?" he asked me, waving his hat at the cloud-black sky. We watched the snow deepen on the limbs of Patrick's tree.

"If you're going to believe at all," he said, "why give up the mystery?"

Patrick was right. It doesn't matter that I can't understand it all, that I'm not even certain I can believe it. With faith, I don't need everything to make sense.

I am still Pentecostal. I can't give up the mystery.

Give 'Em Jesus

EVERY FEW HOURS ON THE FLIGHTS AND layovers from Huntington, West Virginia, to Port-au-Prince, Haiti, the girls in my teen mission group from New Life Victory Center raised their fists and shrieked, "Let's give 'em Jesus!" I was too shy to join in the battle cry, but I shared the sentiment. Jesus I certainly had: journal entries from those years read like grateful, penitent prayers to my sole, omniscient Reader. I was burning to pass Him on.

After my salvation experience at age four, bundled in a cold car, repeating a prayer after my mother, I began shoving a pink New Testament at relatives who seemed suspiciously sinful. "You need to read this," I admonished my devout grandpa, who smoked in his vegetable garden and skipped church.

As I grew, my fervor increased, but I became quiet and bookish. The weekly chapel sermons about witnessing at Grace Christian School left me inspired and terrified. One morning, my fourth-grade teacher placed a neat stack of tracts on each particleboard desk, ordering us to promise we'd pass them out in our neighborhoods. That night, I stood in my gravel driveway and hurled the cards into a stiff wind, praying lost souls would find them.

In high school at Grace Christian, the teachers' witnessing guilt trips intensified. The students had reached the "age of accountability," or outgrown the free passes to Heaven for children who die too young to comprehend the Gospel. Responsible now for our own souls, it was time to shoulder the souls of others. In classes for every subject—Bible, biology, English, American history—we studied Jesus's Great Commission and watched inspirational videos. On screen, hundreds of clocks ticked at once, symbolizing the moments that remained before sinners slipped into Hell. Every afternoon, I went home energized and guilty: I just *had* to win souls for the Lord.

But sinful souls can be elusive. I didn't have any of those "unsaved friends" we were supposed to witness to; I'd met my mall and telephone buddies at school or church. I shyly harassed strangers at libraries and piano recitals, but it never seemed to do any good. Winning souls just wasn't as easy as winning a game of Bible Trivia, even when I attacked my victims with a step-by-step procedure. *First, you share something personal, so they feel comfortable opening up to you . . .* Even if I succeeded, and one scroungy sinner showed up in church the next Sunday, there were just too many more who needed saving.

The week before my mission trip, my tenth-grade geography teacher, a fervent red-haired woman in her midtwenties, shared her personal burden of witnessing shame. She'd popped a tire on her Volvo on a dark country road, and a young man had stopped to help her. She'd spoken with the man about her love for Jesus, but, she confessed, tears in her blue eyes, "I didn't witness to him. When I get to Heaven, if that man's not there, I'll know it's on my hands."

The story scared me. What was the difference between talking about Jesus and "witnessing"? Was I even doing it right? When I entered the pearly gates, would a single person grasp my hand, sobbing, and say she'd made it to Heaven because of me?

I needed to do something big for Jesus, and Haiti seemed like the answer. Traveling abroad, carrying the good news to peasants and factory workers who practiced voodoo: this trip was my chance to store up treasure in Heaven.

+ + +

Standing in the concrete-floored airport in Port-au-Prince, my skirt and blouse rumpled from travel, I waited in line to receive a stamp on my brand-new passport. I reached the desk, a gray metal affair in a five-by-five-foot room, and a woman stamped at random a blue page without speaking. Her skin was dark as black coffee, more like the African converts who accompanied fund-raising missionaries from church to church than my mocha-tinted friend Brianna, the only nonwhite member of our twenty-person expedition.

The airport was nearly empty, and American tourists in flip-flops, ready for a tan on their pale feet, outnumbered the black airport workers. But with that stamp I felt the pallor of my skin. I sensed the teeming dark people beyond the walls, and I knew we were going to stand out.

I was prepared. I'd read about the country's 95 percent black population, descendants of a successful slave uprising in 1791 that established Haiti as the first free black republic. Still, the feeling was startling. My part of southwestern West Virginia had few people of color. To my sixteen-year-old self, Huntington's African American residents seemed limited to a few suit-wearing members of New Life Victory Center and tired mothers who fanned themselves on their front steps while their children played, either in the projects or a few blocks of near-condemned houses smaller than trailers, painted in garish shades of blue, red, and green.

I realize now that the situation is far more complex. Many of Huntington's black residents still live on the streets around the shut-down Barnett Elementary School and Douglass High School, architectural relics of the days when my grandparents watched *Snow White and the Seven Dwarfs* on the main floor of the theater and "coloreds" sat up in the balcony. However, a few years ago, my mother had a black gynecologist, who likely lived among Huntington's wealthier whites in a neighborhood on a hill. The receptionist lowered her voice when my mother made the appointment. "He's black," she whispered into the phone. "I don't care," my mother said. "Well, I had to tell you," the receptionist replied. "A lot of women care." A black male inspecting their vaginas must be more than those women can bear.

My parents raised me not to feel superior to Huntington's black residents because of skin color or money—we had white relatives in the projects, after all—but it was impossible to keep away from well-meaning, racist people. For track and field practices, Grace Christian borrowed an outdoor facility two blocks from old Douglass High School. A rusted fence and a shabby rainbow of dwellings surrounded the field. My high school track coach, a skinny, pale man with thinning brown hair, warned the team to be wary of the neighborhood's dark-skinned inhabitants. "If you see any black folks around here, keep walking, and never, never look them in the eye," he said. "They might have a gun, and you might not even see it." My coach was as zealous as anyone at Grace Christian, reciting scripture as we pushed our panting bodies around the asphalt track, but safety, and prejudice, came before witnessing.

One day during practice, three little boys approached the fence with a kickball. When the boys saw the all-white students running in circles, they stopped and stared. I waved as I ran, and the tiniest boy poked his nose through the chicken wire and smiled. It was *their* field, so I hoped the coach would tell them we'd soon be loading the bus and driving away. The coach ignored them, fixing his eyes on the track. The boy with the kickball grabbed the toddler's hand, and they turned and walked back down the street.

+ + +

A pair of missionaries from West Virginia picked us up at the airport. The plump, pink-skinned, gray-haired couple had lived in Haiti on and off for two decades, establishing churches, a clinic, and a school. Pastor Paul pulled up in an SUV with plush seats and air-conditioning; his wife Betty drove a blue pickup. "Climb into the back with your suitcases!" Betty called, motioning toward the truck bed.

For most of my Haitian journeys, I joggled along in Betty's truck bed, arriving at churches and mountain villages with matted hair and a layer of dirt that darkened my skin. But on that first trip to the missionary compound in Delmas, I ended up in the SUV, barreling up and down hills on a paved narrow snarl. "Don't be scared! These roads take some getting used to," Pastor Paul said, stomping the brake as a car with flat green paint careened around us on a blind curve. "Nobody's got drivers' licenses here. Most people here can't read, anyway, so if they had a test, no one would be able to drive."

Anna, Pastor Garrett's daughter, interrupted the nervous teenage laughter to ask what we'd be doing that week. A confident, brown-eyed beauty, Anna planned to be a missionary herself one day. Pastor Paul coughed, and I leaned forward in my seat, expectant. I'd heard about mission trips to Mexico and South America from other students at school. Those teenagers had built houses, placed old eyeglasses on a table so villagers could try on pair after pair until their children's faces came into focus, their lips and eyelashes distinct for the first time. "We'll visit some villages, a few of our churches, and on Wednesday we'll take you to the clinic," Pastor Paul said. I smiled, picturing myself cuddling emaciated children and bandaging wounds. "And I'm sure Betty'll want to take you kids out for some fun— like the beach and some shopping."

Pastor Paul chuckled as he slowed for a flock of chickens that were ambling across the road. "Welcome to Haiti," he said, watching our faces in the rearview mirror. Runaway chickens didn't seem so exclusively Haitian to me. I'd seen fighting cocks a mile from my house, tethered to blue barrels in otherwise respectable front yards, and I didn't know yet that Haitian churchgoers didn't bother to shoo the chickens when they wandered into a Sunday service.

As Pastor Paul drove through Port-au-Prince, we snapped pictures of upper-class dwellings with creamy stucco walls and scarlet roofs. I considered these houses far prettier than the brick monstrosities the Huntington elite preferred. Then we spotted tangled networks of thin wire that twisted around tree branches and drooped across the street. Pastor Paul explained that the city's poorer residents used these metal spider webs to steal electricity from businesses and the wealthy.

The electricity thieves must have been better off than most, able to afford bulbs to burn. As we moved away from the city, there was light only by day in the homes we passed: one-room buildings, some of them left incomplete until their inhabitants could afford to buy more concrete blocks. On the dirt near the houses, barefoot little girls sat with their floral dresses unbuttoned down the backs, seeking relief from the heat. So much poverty, so many people to reach. "Welcome to Haiti," I murmured to myself.

+ + +

FROM the outside, the missionary compound reminded me of the biblical city of Jericho: tall, white walls surrounded gray, flat-roofed buildings. I imagined Israelites marching with trumpets. Inside the compound, a private generator powered the central air, and water for hand washing flowed from chrome spigots. The water wasn't up to American drinking standards, so we filled Dixie cups from an imported water cooler when we brushed our teeth.

The bunk beds were soft and the food was good, but it took me less than twenty-four hours to feel uncomfortable in the compound. The missionaries had sent us pamphlets to peruse before we arrived, informing us about the language (Haitian Creole) and the currency (gourdes), and they'd instructed female group members to pack skirts, as Haitians would take offense if we wore pants. Haitians are a dressy people, despite their poverty; I saw women in skirts working in the fields. The skirt rule didn't bother me—I had to wear skirts to school every day—but I was embarrassed and dismayed to find more at stake in this dress code than establishing cultural rapport.

To get from the bathroom to the room where I slept, I had to walk through the common room where we prayed and ate. On my first night at the compound, I showered and dressed for bed in the bathroom—modest shorts and a T-shirt—and hurried across the common area, my sweat-stained skirt and blouse in hand. There wasn't a Haitian convert in sight. The next day, a fellow female traveler warned me, "Pastor Paul saw you last night, and he was upset. You have to put your skirt back on when you leave the bathroom."

"Really?" I said, annoyed. "It's ten feet. I can't believe it matters."

"It's the rules," the girl said. "I always take mine with me."

Seething, my face and neck red, I rushed to my bunk to hide and recover. The skirts were for Pastor Paul, not the Haitians.

Shower time was uncomfortable, but mealtime was even worse. Haitian servants waited on us. "It's a kindness to them. Haitians need employment," Pastor Paul said as a dark-skinned woman in an apron set a bowl of mashed potatoes on the dinner table. She and several other women cooked, served us at meals, and did our laundry, removing stains from a blouse I'd long given up on. When an arm appeared over my shoulder at dinner to refill my glass of orange-banana juice, I felt like I was living in one of the classic movies I'd watched with my mother. Not quite *Gone with the Wind*, but one made and set in the 1940s, with the lovable black cooks and housekeepers every white middle-class family seemed ready to exploit.

+ + +

BY my second day in Haiti, I was impatient to be a blessing, so I rose before the dawn alarm clock and put on a skirt, ready to take my place in the truck bed. When we left for the day, I discovered an immediate difference from riding in the SUV, one that distracted me from calculating the number of strands of long thin hair I'd lose in my brush that night. Not only could I see the people as they lived and laughed and worked, *they* could see *us*. They looked up at our freckled faces as we passed by: a teenage boy washing a muddy bicycle, a child taking a drink of water, a woman scrubbing clothes on a rock, all in the same shallow stream. Children in the fields dropped their hoes and waved with both hands, their smiles bright under rows of braids.

The children's friendliness charmed me; I wanted to speak to them. We stopped at a village: ten beige, concrete houses surrounding one outhouse with corrugated metal walls. I approached a child and smiled. She lowered her head and clutched her skirt. "Hi," I said, waving. The little girl waved back. Pastor Paul and Betty had assured us the children knew no English, but I tried anyway. "I'm Sarah Beth. What's your name?"

The little girl shook her head in tearful frustration, responding with what might have been the only English she knew. "Don't understand." Wanting to fix my mistake, I tried Spanish, reasoning that Haitian Creole had French roots, and both French and Spanish came from Latin, but she just repeated her plea, "Don't understand."

The teenagers in my group who'd taken high school French fared a little better, finding a few words in their limited vocabulary that corresponded to the Haitian lexicon. I asked Anna, who knew some French, for something I could say. "*Foto*," she said. "They love to have their picture taken. You don't even have to take it. Just make it look like you did." In demonstration, Anna held her camera up in front of her face. "*Foto?*" Children all around us posed, their bare toes curling in the dirt. She chose a child at random and snapped a picture; the little girl tilted her head, spread her skirt with her hands, and smiled. *Foto* was a word I knew; it sounded like English, and it was spelled the same in Haitian Creole, Spanish, and French. My album from Haiti is full of such *fotos:* children smiling at the thought of pictures of themselves they'd never see.

There were a few Haitian people we could talk to, adults who had worked closely with Pastor Paul and Betty and learned English. A man we called Pastor Edner joined us in the back of the truck, captivating his little audience with his explosive laugh. He laughed hardest when Anna told him about her pet cat at home. Hunting their own food, constantly breeding, cats are a popular form of meat in Haiti. "A cat!" he cried, clapping his hands over his head and guffawing. "You mean you like it for your friend?"

I saw Pastor Edner's cats when we visited his house: scruffy beasts that crouched inside doorways, their ears notched in ownership. I wished I could smuggle the cats home in my suitcase, but far more haunting was the pride that radiated from the Haitian preacher's face as he gave us a tour. From the outside, the house looked like the others in the hilltop village, concrete blocks with a slanting metal roof, but these blocks concealed jewels: rooms. One wall separated the bed where Pastor Edner slept beside his wife—a mattress and a discount-store comforter on the dirt floor—from the identical bed where four of his children slept, and another wall created a space for a spindly wood table.

"This house is really nice," Pastor Paul hissed behind our heads as a reminder to compliment. We smiled and took pictures. I thought of the cramped bedroom I shared with Jennifer; I hadn't realized how large it was.

At the end of the day, we returned to the compound and refreshed ourselves with homemade pizza and orange-banana juice. Then we took turns showering, rinsing away the dirt we'd picked up in the village, watching our encounter with third-world poverty scurry down the drain.

✢ ✢ ✢

The day before we flew back to West Virginia, Betty took us out for her promised "fun day." A day that made me suspect none of us understood Haiti. As we packed up our swimsuits and piled into the truck and SUV, we suddenly weren't missionaries at all, but vacationers in the Caribbean.

Our first stop was shopping in the streets of downtown Port-au-Prince, seeking mementos to set on our bedroom dressers and to give to family and friends. Street vendors assailed us from all sides, holding out necklaces of mahogany-stained seeds and pointing out bright racks of landscape paintings, embroidered clothing, and hand-carved wooden animals. At first, I wanted to buy everything and pay as much as I possibly could, thinking of the poverty the sellers likely endured. But soon I got caught up in haggling, seeking to pay as few gourdes as possible for a red-and-green carved duck for my dad, necklaces and maracas for my siblings, a woven basket purse for me. Haiti would soon exist for me only in pictures and scrawled journal entries; I wanted something tangible to show for my journey. Souvenirs in hand, we climbed back into the vehicles and rode to the Caribbean coast.

The beach we visited belonged to an exclusive tourist resort: clean white sand, banana trees, exotic pink flowers, hardly any people. I'd seen the same flora elsewhere in Haiti—lining the roadside, in between farms—here arranged for the enjoyment of white tourists. A tall brown wall separated the resort from what I considered the *real* Haiti: street vendors hawking carved giraffes, barefoot boys on bicycles, a clutch of women laughing in a dirt front yard.

The resort wall reminded me of the floodwall that divides my hometown from the Ohio and Guyandotte Rivers. Huntington built its wall after the 1937 flood, when my dad's mother and her nine siblings stepped through a second-story window into a rowboat. Huntington's wall serves its residents; it protects basements during rainstorms and gives little boys a quiet place to fish. The wall in Haiti keeps the residents from dirtying the beach and protects tourists from seeing anything unpleasant. If a rich white couple saw a dusty child in a ripped dress, they might go elsewhere for their next vacation.

To get into the resort, Pastor Paul and Betty showed membership cards at a window and a gate opened in the wall. Inside, we lunched at an outdoor café—picnic tables on a covered wooden deck—and ordered hamburgers, lobster, and shrimp. Then we changed into swimsuits, the one-pieces Pastor Paul required, and waded and swam in the clear blue sea.

I looked at the strangers on the beach around me. A few Haitians, waiting tables or selling shells and dried starfish, and a few tourists, likely Americans. One elderly man had a bright blue Speedo and pasty veined legs. At that point, I'd been in Haiti for five days. I'd used the filthy outhouses, sat in a hard chair as Pastor Edner preached in Haitian Creole, and I imagined I understood the people, their culture, their poverty. It hurt me to realize I had more in common with the old man in a Speedo. He sunned his white skin on his thick towel, blissfully ignoring the pain beyond the wall.

+ + +

AFTER I went back home, I reflected in my journal, "The Haiti trip was awesome. A greater blessing is hard to imagine." If I'd been more honest, I would have written that when it came to witnessing, really reaching out to the lost, the trip was a disappointment. I'd added no riches to my Heavenly treasure pile. My enjoyment of the trip was more sensual than spiritual: snowy mountains of clouds through airplane windows, summer sun in April, the blue water of the Caribbean washing my hot feet, maracas accompanying Haitian voices through the uncertain sounds of a memorized American hymn.

We'd done everything Pastor Paul had promised that first day in the SUV: traveled to villages, churches, and the clinic.

But we could barely communicate with the people, and there was never anything for us to do. Throughout the week, I stood awkwardly, watching and waiting as Betty dispensed medicine, as Pastor Paul preached. It was a visit, not a mission. My only contributions to the Haitian people were the sticks of gum I'd passed out to children at the clinic; a skirt and blouse I'd brought in my suitcase; and a short, hesitant sermon, delivered through a translator to a church of devoted believers—literally preaching to the faithful.

I'd failed to realize the trip wasn't for the Haitians at all, but for ourselves. Before the trip, a woman at New Life Victory Center had prophesied to the mothers of the teenage girls in the mission group. "It will be a life-changing spiritual experience," she'd said. "You won't know your girls when they come back." We went not to help, but to see the poverty, to solidify our evangelical fervor, to feel as cocky white Americans *we could* "make a difference."

The Sunday after we got home, our sunburned mission team clustered around the glass pulpit, waiting for the opportunity to testify. "These kids have sure fulfilled the Great Commission," Pastor Garrett joked by way of an introduction. "They've taken Jesus to the 'uttermost part of the earth.'" Frozen by the thousand church members who gazed up at us from their cushioned chairs, I smiled stiffly at the back of the group, hoping no one would notice me. Brianna stepped forward, certain of what she should say. "Before I went to Haiti, I felt so dry in my walk with the Lord," she said. "Now that's far behind me."

Dry. I whispered the word, mulling it over. I'd never felt that way. I figured it was something only a public school student could feel, someone exposed daily to the temptations of sex and cigarettes. In comparison to my friend, glowing with her newfound spiritual damp, I felt my Haitian experience had been a failure.

At Brianna's words, the congregation cheered, standing and throwing their hands in the air in worshipful ecstasy. "Praise the Lord!" they shouted. It was official: our trip had been successful, though we'd really accomplished nothing. We'd left the Haitians behind to eat cat, to live their entire lives without flushing a toilet, to swish their dusty skirts—a swirl of scarlet, emerald, indigo, tangerine—as they danced their voodoo ceremonies. But none of that mattered. *Our* lives would never be the same.

✢ ✢ ✢

MORE than a decade has passed since my trip to Haiti, and I've gotten over most of my guilt about witnessing. I've realized the best Christianity lies simply in living, and it's far better to give strangers sincere, inconspicuous help—a spare dollar at a checkout counter, a tire change on a dark country road—than to ask them questions about their souls.

And I've realized that in some respects, my trip wasn't a failure at all. Before I went to Haiti, I'd never been on an airplane, and the closest I'd come to foreign travel was visiting the Australia exhibit at the Cincinnati Zoo. The prophesying churchwoman was right: I wasn't the same when I came back. I'd read about the poverty in Haiti, but it didn't touch me until I studied the stream-washed faces: pride in a concrete house, joy in a hymn, determination to get more gourdes for a string of beads that would snap on a tourist's trip home. When my old car needs repairs or a check bounces at the bank, I can conjure up these faces and try to feel grateful.

A year after my trip, and a few months before my family left New Life Victory Center, Pastor Paul and Betty paid the church a fund-raising visit. I was excited to hear Pastor Paul talk, though I hadn't particularly liked him; I wanted to hear about Haiti, the people I'd met and left behind. He didn't mention them.

"Women should be *submissive*," he said, leaning his broad face across the pulpit. "Take my wife Betty, for example. She does what I tell her to, and she never complains. If there's anything I can't stand it's a yapping woman." Betty stood beside Pastor Paul at the pulpit; he thumped her back, and she stared at the floor. I noticed my mother's neck reddening beside me, and I sank lower in my seat. I knew what was coming, and I was thankful our seats were at the back of the sanctuary. My mother hadn't raised me to think people inferior in terms of gender any more than race.

"All right," my mother yelled. "But I don't want any yapping man!"

I fought the urge to get up and run, and as soon as I dared I escaped to the bathroom, praying I wouldn't see anyone I knew. It hit me then that Pastor Paul reveled in the dressiness of Haitian culture, using it as an excuse to impose his opinions on American women.

+ + +

ON a long mountain drive to a Haitian village, our group got out to stretch our muscles in a graveyard, the site of weekly voodoo drumming, dances, and chants. Pastor Paul and Betty cringed as they described the ritual. Secretly, I wished we could have watched it. Gifts to spirits and ancestors blanketed the graveyard: homemade bread on a gravestone, a slice of a goat's head nailed to a tree.

A starving white cow, its hipbones like handles, wandered in and paused next to me as I stood, drinking Pepsi from a glass bottle. Pitying the cow, I picked up the bread from the gravestone and held it out, an offering. The animal moaned and trotted away.

Hot Girls in Short Skirts

A BOY WHO GELLED HIS HAIR WITH SPIT was once in love with me. For gym class, Brandon buckled a train engine belt over his sweatpants. He had chronic diarrhea; he'd suffer in the restroom until he'd exhausted the toilet paper supply, then he'd come back to class and ask the teacher to alert the janitor. From the fourth to sixth grades, Brandon loved me, and one day in the school library, he tried to ask me out.

Brandon didn't know what to say. He began by insisting the other boys had lied: he didn't want to "get in bed" with me. This was the first I'd heard of this rumor, and even Brandon's denial made me queasy. As a fundamentalist fifth grader at Grace Christian School, my ideas about getting in bed with someone were fuzzy, but I understood that "in bed" meant sin. And the idea of Brandon creeping under my Holly Hobby quilt and laying his spitty head on my pillow was too much to bear. I knew what I had to do.

I dropped my books and slammed Brandon against a bookshelf; *Paddington Bear* and *Nancy Drew* rained around him. Brandon was larger than I was, but I knew he wouldn't hit a girl, and he liked me too much to tell a teacher.

"In bed with me?" I hissed, too softly for the librarian to hear.

"I promise, I never said that!" he pleaded, almost in tears. But I wouldn't listen. I dug my fingernails into his arms until he bled.

I knew I was being cruel, but I really had to hurt him. My family couldn't afford the Myrtle Beach vacations the other kids bragged about, and I wore plaid jumpers my granny had made. If I'd been polite to Brandon, I would have been admitting he was an equal, that I was no better than a train-belt freak. On the way back to class, the girls gave me sympathetic hugs, and the boys high-fived me for my bravery. Brandon walked at the back of the group, another boy punching the air beside his head.

+ + +

YEARS before I pinched Brandon, I liked to play with my mother's high school yearbook. I imagined the black-and-white people styling through the Huntington streets in their bell-bottoms and wide ties, chatting their way to Burger Chef from Huntington East High School. With a little help from my mother, it was easy to tell the somebodies from the students who might have belted their sweatpants. The majorettes had hair like corn silk that stopped just below their full breasts. Awe crept into my mother's voice when she pointed these girls out. The dorky students—male and female—had halos of untamable frizz. Popularity, it seemed, lay in the genes.

My mother's photo fascinated me most. Like me, she seemed to rank somewhere in between: not the sort who'd inform the class about her diarrhea, but not majorette material, either. In the picture, she holds her lips in a tight line, hiding her braces. She looks quiet and small. Her long dark hair curtains around her face in soft waves.

When I was little, I enjoyed crayoning pictures of myself as an adult, and I often based my prophetic creations on that picture. Matching my colors to the blacks and grays, I darkened my tea-tinted hair to umber and sealed my pink lips tight. As I traced the rumpled lines of my grown-up hair, I noticed a discrepancy between the soft waves in the yearbook picture and my mother's natural tangle of curls. "I ironed it," she told me. "I ironed it on the ironing board and burned myself to pieces. And look at that picture—my hair still wouldn't lie flat." My mother showed me a scar: an inch-long white streak on her left forearm.

I imagined that burn fresh and livid, my mother's tears as she finished flattening her hair, her grimace as she tugged on her jeans.

✦   ✦   ✦

RALPH married twice—two equally fiery women—and the marriages began and ended the same way. The first time around, he was engaged to Dot. They'd fought the whole time they were dating; Ralph realized the marriage was a bad idea. And one day, on a porch swing, he broke off the engagement. "I just can't do it, Dot," he said.

Dot wrapped her arms around Ralph and bawled into his collar, smearing his shoulder with lipstick. He couldn't abandon her and Lee, her eight-year-old boy. Ralph had no idea then how Dot's first marriage had ended. That her husband had asked a female friend to lie down with him, wrapped in his and Dot's sheets, at a time he knew his wife would catch them. Ralph saw a woman in love, her nose red with terror. He kissed Dot to comfort her, and as he confessed to my mother just before he died: "Marcy, we ended up in bed." It was the 1950s, and Ralph was decent, so he married her.

After thirteen years of smashed dishes and rare slaps, Ralph and Dot had a spectacular row, and Ralph carried a newspaper out to the porch to cool off. She locked him out, and he rode the city bus to his mother's house. Dot changed her mind a few months later, but Ralph's sister Louava intervened. She worked at a lawyer's office, and she wrote a letter on her employer's letterhead, warning Dot to leave Ralph alone. Dot lived in awe of anything legal, so, frightened, she obeyed.

The second time around, Ralph was engaged to a loud woman named Bernadine. She was gorgeous for her age by 1970s standards, with a bright blond beehive and turquoise eye shadow. Bernadine called incapable people "one-armed wallpaper hangers" and her ex-husband "the Great White Father." When she went to the restroom, she quipped, "Where's the litter box? This cat's gotta go!"

Again, Ralph quarreled with his fiancée, and this time, he was determined to escape. He spent a day at Camden Park with Bernadine and her daughters, two slim, dark-eyed girls with brown corn-silk hair. Sharon was sixteen, a year older than Marcy. Kim was nine. On the Wild West train ride, the women sandwiched Ralph on one narrow bench: Bernadine on his right, her daughters on the left. The girls stared at the train car's ceiling and picked at their nails, too old to scream when the plastic cowboys massacred the plastic Indians. "Why don't you tell us about driving real trains, Ralph?" said Bernadine. "And those free train tickets you can get for *family*." She punctuated *family* with a squeeze on Ralph's knee.

"Oh, the girls have heard all that stuff before," Ralph said, his leg stiffening. They *had* heard it before. The cross-country train trip Ralph's sisters took when they were young, hot-potato-passing the enormous basket of fried chicken their mother had forced into their hands as they left. The time Ralph wrecked, and the locomotive escaped the tracks and plunged into the weeds. Ralph didn't have the heart to tell those stories again. He knew it was time to say good-bye.

That evening, Ralph dropped Bernadine off at home, and he told her the engagement was over. Bernadine didn't wail like Dot, and Ralph managed to slink back to his car. Then, as he backed out of the driveway, Sharon ran out, tears flowing. "We love you, Ralph," she told him. "You have to marry Mama. Please!" Ralph melted. He let Sharon take his hand and lead him back inside.

Nine years later, Ralph and Bernadine had a spectacular row, and Ralph carried a newspaper out to the porch to cool off. Bernadine locked the doors and called his mother to come pick him up.

Bernadine tried to hold Ralph's belongings hostage, but his sister Anita came to the rescue. She dragged her sheepish brother onto the front porch of the house he still owned and banged on the door. Anita said, "Honey, you're going to let us in, and you're letting us walk right back out."

✦   ✦   ✦

BRANDON wasn't the only boy who liked me in late elementary. Zoltan inked his name and mine on a fencepost behind the school. Zack showed me his hand-colored Superman symbols, hoping I'd approve his crayon box selections of reds, yellows, and blues. Mark and I shook our chocolate milk cartons at lunch, seeing who could make the best milkshake. I proofread the mystery novel Shawn was writing and met up with him at the mall bookstore. Shawn added a scene to his novel where a boy like him kissed a girl like me.

✦   ✦   ✦

FROM the Grace Christian School Handbook, as I remember it:

- Earrings on young men imply ungodliness, homosexuality, and dirt. Young ladies with more than two earrings are likely to become pregnant.

- When a young lady drops to her knees, her skirt must be long enough to brush the floor. Young ladies cannot understand what their bare knees do to male teachers. Both shoulders must be covered, and not a hint of breast must show. A church is the Lord's house, and this school is His workplace.

- If three male students enter an empty room carrying a guitar, a drum set, a keyboard, and an amp, they have invited the devil.

- Be sure your immorality will find you out, especially if you are female. Girls wearing jackets, then peacoats, then parkas to class rarely pass for virgins in their graduation gowns.

- The administration is aware that at our sister school, students waltz to *Blue Danube* and *Tales from the Vienna Woods* at their version of a prom, the black tuxes a modest distance from the pastel tulle. But we've seen hands touching shoulders, hands touching waists, legs rhythmically jigging. Young men must preserve perfect purity of thought, and Strauss is not worth the risk.

- Note that the above regulations are not meant to keep order in the school, but to foster holiness in the students' lives. A boy who careens his bicycle past the principal and his terrier in June, chrome and earrings glinting, will pay the price in August.

- Note further that the above offenses are not infractions, but sins against God. The lust of the flesh, the lust of the eyes, and the pride of life.

✣ ✣ ✣

HUNTINGTON East High School's mascot was a Highlander. Students voted in the tartan-clad clansman in the 1940s, possibly because of Huntington's large Scots-Irish population, and possibly because "Highlander" puns so cutely off of "high school." The 1940s majorettes ordered wool uniforms from Scotland in maroon-and-gold plaid: a hat with a feather, a Miss America-style sash, and a kilt so tiny the girls' underwear shows in the yearbook photos. In the 1970s, the majorettes donned these vintage outfits and kicked and twirled to "The Bonnie Lassie," the Ames Brothers' sped-up version of "Scotland the Brave."

Grace Christian School's mascot was a Soldier, taken by the school's founders from Second Timothy, chapter 2, verse 4. "No man that warreth entangleth himself with the affairs of this life; that he may please Him who hath chosen him to be a soldier." Soldiers battled basketball teams, and Soldiers battled sin. "Onward Christian Soldiers" was our fight song. To avoid the appearance of dancing, our cheerleaders held their knees straight and stiff. They looked like soldiers themselves, "marching as to war, with the cross of Jesus going on before."

Like their public school counterparts, Soldier cheerleaders covered their bras and stomachs with polyester shells. Orangey gold and royal blue. But they concealed their arms and necks with a white turtleneck bodysuit. Soldier cheerleaders wore the usual polyester skirts, special ordered so the pleats would reach their knees. One of those polyester-encased girls claimed, her smile smug with secret knowledge, that the Soldiers played better with the cheerleaders on the sidelines. She said, "Boys like hot girls in short skirts."

+ + +

IN high school, Marcy loved Andy Jones, football player and high school chaplain. I'm sure she found Andy's pregame prayers as attractive as his football jersey. With his shaggy brown hair and nut-brown eyes, Andy looked a little like Lynn Whiting, the godlike Romeo in the 1968 *Romeo and Juliet*. My mom can still recite much of that movie's script.

One Saturday, at a public pool, Marcy spread out a quilt on the grass, ready to bake her ivory skin. She left to buy a Coke, and when she came back, there was Andy in the middle of her blanket. He'd propped his dripping body on his muscular arms and dangled one long leg onto the grass. A bevy of sleek-haired majorettes surrounded him, elbowing each other for more space on the quilt. Marcy sipped her Coke on the grass a few feet away, feeling more honored than put out. She'd left a comb by her blanket, and Andy found it. Grinning at a favorite majorette, he combed the chlorine from his hair.

That night, alone, Marcy hugged that blanket and combed her hair until it hurt.

+ + +

RALPH wanted so badly for his stepdaughters to love him.

He took Bernadine, Sharon, and Kim on vacations to Myrtle Beach; he'd taken his first family to murky Dreamland Pool. Marcy tagged along on a beach trip, but it wasn't the same. Ralph hated pierced ears and asked Marcy to promise never to get them. He paid for Sharon's and Kim's piercings and purchased their studs. When Marcy got married, Ralph bought a used wedding dress from the preacher's wife, out of style and so short Marcy had to walk down the aisle without shoes. Sharon picked out a new dress at a bridal shop and had it tailored to fit her curves. Ralph paid. And the kicker, the atrocity my mother grumbled about as she drove me to school: Ralph paid for Kim's majorette lessons. Marcy had asked her father for the lessons a few years before, and he'd told her he couldn't afford them. His financial situation hadn't changed. Kim made the squad, and Marcy had not.

Ralph knew Marcy loved him, so he could be himself around her. His Great Depression–warped, cheap-bastard self.

+ + +

THE closest thing my school had to majorette lessons was cheerleading camp. Nearly every girl in the elementary school signed up. Thirty dollars bought one long Saturday in the school gym and a cheap blue T-shirt with a gold incantation: *Cheer! Cheer! Cheer!* The cheerleaders were raising money to go to a real camp in Florida.

I knew the cheerleaders from the pep rallies, those breath-taking pregame performances that sometimes freed my class from an afternoon science lesson. On a blue-carpeted platform in the school gym, the cheerleaders jumped and yelled, their arms a flurry of blue-and-gold pompoms. A high school boy in a pink Energizer Bunny suit interrupted the performance: "The Soldiers keep going and going and going!" My kindergarten sister Jennifer got so excited she peed all over her folding chair.

The cheerleaders showed up to the Saturday camp in pep rally regalia: heavy makeup and those glamorous uniforms. They let us touch their pompoms if we were careful. Seeing the cheerleaders up close in their full glory was worth at least half the camp's cost.

At the camp, each cheerleader marshaled five little girls and taught us a Soldiers cheer. When the day ended, the returning mothers in their Saturday jean skirts clustered in the back of the gym. I stood in front of the real cheerleaders, flailing my arms and bungling my steps, and the embers of my mom's dreams ignited again.

+ + +

WITH the end of the sixth grade came cheerleading tryouts. In August, my class would be moving down the hall, into the world of locker combinations, daily chapel, and teenage girls who snapped "Hurry up, little girl" when I took too long in the bathroom. It would be so much easier to face that world armed with a set of pompoms.

Of the eight girls in my class, seven of us practiced our kicks and jumps. All but Ruth Ann, whose parents couldn't afford the next year's costlier junior high tuition. I whispered with the other girls that Ruth Ann wouldn't have made it, anyway. She was tall and fat, her blond hair was short and droopy, and her mother made her jumpers. She also made straight As and beat the boys at basketball, but that didn't matter right then.

I was hopeful. I weighed 63 pounds—perfect for climbing female pyramids and rocketing into the air as a flyer—and I still had my T-shirt from cheerleading camp. When the coach asked us to write our own cheers, I figured I had those tryouts in the bag. I spent an evening on my bed with a sheet of notebook paper, comparing Soldiers to natural disasters. "We'll knock you down like a hurricane," I muttered, staring down my Cabbage Patch dolls. I drew skirted stickmen in the margins, their penciled limbs wobbling along with my rhymes.

My confidence wilted partway through the practice week when two new girls showed up. They'd be joining our class the next year. Rachel had a smile that outshone her bat ears and stringy, waist-length black hair. Kitty had perfect bangs and a belch that echoed in the gym's rafters. These new girls didn't have cheerleading camp T-shirts, and mine suddenly felt faded and limp. I sent my mom to Kmart for a gold T-shirt and blue shorts.

When the tryout day came, my mom curled my ponytail and ironed my new shirt. "You're beautiful. You look like a cheerleader," she told me. She beamed her hazel eyes into the bathroom mirror, connecting with my blue-green. For that moment, I believed her.

I tried out in the gym with the other sixth-grade hopefuls. The cheerleading coach and two women with teased hair frowned at us from a table. Without the recess din of shouts and bouncing four-squares, I could hear the eerie hum of the air conditioner. One by one, we jumped: herkie, toe-touch, pike. My legs hovered near the ground on the toe-touch, but I managed to land on my feet. Then the group performed a short cheer we'd learned at tryouts, and that was it. My stick figures pouted in my pocket.

The next day, a gold sheet framed in blue glitter appeared on the wall in the hallway. Kitty and Rachel had made it, and the rest of my class had not. I sobbed into my book bag on the car ride home.

I wondered if the judges had seen me in my own homemade jumpers. Brown-and-orange plaid that resembled the waitresses' uniform at the hot dog drive-in. Red plaid I'd worn proudly until Shawn had told me I looked like a mama's girl. Flimsy, pale turquoise from an enormous bolt Granny had found on sale. "We can't waste it, honey, but you can pick out some new fabric after I use all this up," Granny consoled me when I complained. I asked her to make my jumpers so long they covered my ankles; surely someday that bolt would run out.

+ + +

IN the seventh grade, Zack threw away his Superman symbols and tried to squeeze Kitty's hand during science lab. Brandon passed Kitty note after note, begging her to meet him at the pop machine. Shawn asked Rachel to marry him, sealing his promise with a cubic zirconia heart. Once after school, Shawn kissed Rachel good-bye; surely he'd noticed me at the picnic table, less than ten feet away. I bit my unkissed lips and managed not to cry.

+ + +

WHEN I tried out, I forgot what I'd learned in the fifth grade, the year I pinched Brandon in the library. I hated cheerleading, and I didn't have what it took.

The six girls in my fifth-grade class organized a squad to cheer for Buddy Basketball, a unisex elementary after-school league coached by high school students. Teams matched their names to the colors of their jerseys: Red, Orange, Light Blue, Navy, Purple, Maroon. Our squad cheered for Maroon because that team had the cutest boys. Nick Joyce gelled his hair with real chemicals, not spit. Shawn looked athletic and powerful without the yellow pencil he kept behind his ear. Brandon was on the Light Blue team, but his jersey wasn't light blue. A yellow highlighter had exploded in his book bag, dyeing his jersey acid green.

A few girls in my class usually joined teams, but at the prospect of cheering, even Ruth Ann stashed her jersey in her closet. We had no uniforms, no coach, and hardly any cheers, but there was something magnetic about the word *cheerleader*. The boys got caught by the magnet, too, dimly understanding that our chants made us sexy. At the basketball games, little male athletes in all colors ogled our maroon T-shirts and mismatched jean skirts, and the Maroon boys swaggered as they dribbled down the court.

Naturally, Megan took charge of the squad. She had the most adult experience—she'd dated Shawn in the third grade when they went to public school—and her severe acne and early period gave her authority with the rest of our pale, unpimpled faces. Megan's mom provided donuts and bottled Kool-Aid, and we practiced every day at recess and for an hour after school. We practiced cheers we'd learned at cheerleading camp, cramming in the phrase "Maroon team" when the real cheer mentioned "Soldiers." And we practiced cheers Megan had learned from public school girls, edited for content after a teacher happened by a practice. "We will, we will . . . beat you!" we thundered, slapping our knees and stomping. "We will rock you" had sounded more menacing, the forbidden word "rock" juicy in our mouths.

In my memory, those months on the Maroon team cheerleading squad feel foreboding, a hint of how miserable I'd be in junior high and high school. When the practices started, I was just another cheerleader, bored but important as anybody. Then the other girls noticed something was wrong with me: I had a voice to match my skinny frame. "Try projecting from your stomach," Megan's mother advised me, but I didn't seem to have a stomach to project from.

One day at recess, the girls got tired of cheering, and they decided to fix my voice instead. Megan plopped down on the bleachers on one side of the gym and ordered me to stand on the other side. There weren't any bleachers over there. I shuffled through the boys' soccer game and huddled against the concrete wall they were using as a goal.

"Now yell, 'Go Maroon team!'" called Megan.

"Go Maroon team!" I flinched on *team*, avoiding a flying ball.

"Yell louder!" Megan's voice boomed across the gym. Cheerleaders were supposed to sound like *that*.

"Go Maroon team!" My throat was starting to hurt.

Nick and Shawn joined the girls on the bleachers, glad to help out their cheerleaders. My whole body felt hot, but I screamed my line again.

"Hey, that was a little bit louder," Nick called, almost kindly. I knew he was lying. My voice was perfect for bossing my siblings, for calling for my beagle when she escaped through the kitchen door, for answering questions about birds in science class. God hadn't designed my voice to cheer on a team.

When Nick and Shawn went back to soccer, Megan stalked across the gym to fetch me. "You can't embarrass the Maroon team," she hissed as I plodded. "If you don't get any better, we're going to make you the mascot." We didn't have a mascot. "The Maroon Monkeys," I'd suggested once, but no one had listened. "The Purple Pelicans," Megan had said. But there really was a Purple team. We'd given up.

We'll make you the mascot. I imagined myself stumbling along in front of the cheerleaders, my body tangled in a shapeless blob of maroon material. My face sweating under something dark and scratchy, my too-quiet voice silenced.

+ + +

SEVENTH grade. Eighth grade. Ninth grade. A gold T-shirt and blue shorts. A blue T-shirt and gold shorts. A white ribbon in my hair. When the coach posted the list, the other hopefuls raced, as if the fastest girl had a better chance of reading her name. Megan finally made the squad; I heard her squeals from a different floor as I stood at my locker, cramming homework into my book bag.

I read the list alone, an hour after school ended. The vacuum hummed louder as the janitor moved into the hallway. I glanced and hurried away so he could clean the carpet under my feet.

+ + +

WHEN I open my mother's high school yearbook to Andy Jones's senior portrait and my own to the face of Nick Joyce, I see eerie similarities. The crooked smile. The dimpled left cheek. Square jaw. Heavy eyebrows. A pleasantly large, down-turned nose. The eye colors are different—Andy's dark, Nick's pale blue—but both pairs reflect the same easy self-confidence: *everyone finds me handsome.* This uncanny resemblance helps me understand why my mother encouraged my futile passion. Maybe I could win where she'd lost, and we'd both feel beautiful and worthy.

Grace Christian School was filled with beat-up pianos; whenever Nick got the chance, he cut class and sat on a piano bench, finding chords that matched the lyrics he'd just written during a lecture. Often, a cheerleader sat beside him, plunking a few notes of her own and pressing her hip into his.

One day, we studied ballads in English class. Mrs. Hall gathered my class around a piano and produced sheet music for "Barbara Allen." A sarcastic woman, close to retirement, the teacher handed the music to Nick. "Why don't you play it for us, Nick?" she crowed. "You're always eager to play the piano." Red-eared, Nick rolled up the music and headed for the bench. Nick never read the novels Mrs. Hall assigned, but I don't think she was being cruel: I don't think she knew he couldn't read music. He blundered through a few bars, and a cheerleader and I both stood up to help. I always read the assigned novels, and I'd placed in statewide classical piano competitions, so the teacher picked me. My classmates sang as I played the melody and Nick accompanied me with his chords.

I could have easily handled the song alone, but I preferred to sit beside Nick, close enough to feel his body heat, our wrists occasionally brushing. "Made every youth cry well-a-day. Her name was Barbara Allen." As we played, my stomach glowed with faint hope; surely I made a better duet partner than those cheerleaders. After class, I approached Nick. He almost never talked to me, and now I had something to say. "That song, it was . . ." Nick grabbed his books and jogged to the lockers.

✣   ✣   ✣

WHEN Marcy was a teenager:

- Lee served in Vietnam. He was only a telephone operator in uniform, connecting generals to colonels and himself to his fiancée. But after the pieces of Dot's sister's son came home—thick, translucent glass covered his smashed nose and lopsided lips at the open-casket viewing—it seemed like Lee might be next. Dot bought a black dress for Lee's funeral and chain-smoked, waiting to hear her son was dead.

- Lee came home, but Dot didn't cheer up.

- Marcy heated freezer-aisle potpies for her and Bobby's dinner, almost forgetting the days when Dot fattened up Ralph with beef stew, macaroni and cheese with canned milk and Colby, her extra-greasy fried chicken.

- Marcy visited Ralph in his big brick house, but she didn't feel at home. She only opened the refrigerator if the silky brown hair and the blond beehive were far away.

- Marcy must have watched the majorettes and hoped. Maybe those kilts from Scotland protected girls from pain.

+ + +

AT my tenth-grade tryouts, I felt more confident than usual as my tennis shoes thudded to the center of the gym. I'd prac- ticed my toe-touch for weeks—gripping a metal beam on the back of the bleachers, hurling both legs toward my head—and a classmate's mother sat at the judging table. The mother had brought strawberry milk and red cupcakes to my elementary school Valentine's Day parties, and I knew she liked me a little. When I nailed my toe-touch, legs perpendicular to my body, my tennis shoes pointed at the walls, I beamed my smile toward that judge's fuzzy brown hair. She smiled back. But then came the group cheer, and I slipped my T-shirt in line with the golds, whites, and blues.

In all of me but my fingers, my kinesthetic memory is poor. My fingers can tackle a Chopin nocturne with ease, but the rest of me stumbles through life. I joined a swing dance club in my midtwenties, hoping to prove I had outgrown my clum- siness and my fundamentalist roots. I hadn't. I blushed when a strange boy held my hand, and I felt naughty when the boy swung my body away from his and tucked me into his arms.

For the first few weeks, it was okay that I was terrible, that I tripped and shuffled when I should have jumped and stepped. "It takes time. You'll get it," the boys reassured me, lowering their balding heads toward my eyes. But more weeks passed, and I did not get it. I slunk away from the dancers one night and never appeared again. On the drive home, I relived my college tennis class when I'd forgotten how to serve the ball, my tenth-grade cheerleading tryouts when I'd forgotten how to move my arms.

During the first half of that group cheer, I stayed in time with the others, a fist up for *Soldier*, both fists down for *blue and gold*, three steps to the right for *win, win, win!* Then came the tricky part—a long sequence of *go* and *fight*—and my arms tangled and yearned to droop at my sides. By stealing a glance at the cheerleader wannabe next to me, I managed to finish with the group. *Don't look at me,* my pink cheeks begged. *I got most of it right.*

"I wish I could rewind that cheer like a videotape," the cupcake woman said. I didn't make the squad.

✦ ✦ ✦

MARCY tried out for the majorette squad in her junior year, the one year her grades were high enough. Since Marcy's salvation at age fifteen, she'd searched the department store racks of tiny skirts for anything long enough to cover her thighs, but she would make an exception for a kilt. In the months before the tryouts, she asked her father for the majorette lessons, and when that failed, she sought help from Lee's wife, Donna.

Donna had *almost* made the majorette squad during her years at Huntington East High School. Her family really had been too poor to pay for majorette lessons, but she'd been popular anyway—football players grinned at her, majorettes spritzed her with their expensive perfume—and she'd possessed enough talent to learn the dances on her own. When Marcy asked for help, Donna put on a record of "The Bonnie Lassie," and they kicked around the living room, performing the steps Donna remembered. Then, in Donna's strip of a backyard, Marcy tossed her silver baton until it stopped smacking her nose.

Tryouts arrived, and Marcy showed up in the school gym with her baton, her hair warm from the ironing board. For a week, she practiced dances with a host of other hopefuls. Fat girls, bucktoothed girls, frizzy-haired girls, girls like my mother who could pass for twelve years old, their training bras flat under their T-shirts. The previous year's majorettes had to try out, too, so for that week, anyone could be glorious.

On tryout day, Marcy entered the gym with a bucktooth, a flat-chest, and one of last year's majorettes, and a judge cued up "The Bonnie Lassie." The girls danced together—three kicks, one baton toss, half of a twirl—and the judge stopped the music. "That'll do," she said. Later that week, a typed list appeared in the hallway, and my mother's name wasn't on it.

When I played with my mother's yearbook, she took the book on her lap and lingered over the majorette pictures. She said, "If the devil himself had appeared with a contract, asking for my soul in exchange for that year on the squad, I would have considered the offer."

+   +   +

IN the eleventh grade, I tried to speak my way onto the cheerleading squad, the way God spoke the moon and mountains into existence. It was my last chance; I needed something stronger than my own poor power. So I followed the example of the biblical woman with an issue of blood. Before the fountain of her blood dried up, she *said*, "If I may touch but His clothes, I shall be whole." As I put on my skirt in the morning, as I prayed over my smashed salami sandwich, as I showered at night, I said, "This year, I will be a cheerleader. I will date Nick."

I reached for Jesus's hem, and the wool slipped from my fingers. My name was missing from the glittery sheet again.

+   +   +

THE reasons I humiliated myself, year after year:

- Cheerleaders rode the bus with the basketball team. During McDonald's stops, they could slide into Nick's booth and steal his French fries. I stood in the parking lot as the bus pulled away, waiting for my mother to drive me home.

- Cheerleaders smiled from a stage at pep rallies, boomed insults down the hallways, brandished earthworms at boys in the biology lab. I lugged a Victorian novel to every class, fearing the teacher would run out of lesson plans and give her students time to chat.

- Cheerleaders had real dates to the Junior-Senior Banquet, our school's dance-free prom. I had a date my senior year: a few philanthropic girls asked me to accompany a plump, freckled, lonely boy who stuttered too badly to form sentences. The girls would have gone with him themselves, of course, but they couldn't abandon their boyfriends. At the banquet, my date and I chewed our twice-baked potatoes in silence. A black-suited man read a passage from the Bible and found a dove in his hat.

- Every time I flung my toes skyward in front of the judges, my mother had another chance.

+ + +

ONCE, when I was in junior high, my mom danced a majorette dance on our stained shag carpet, humming "The Bonnie Lassie" in sync with her flying limbs. Twenty years after her failed tryout, she remembered every kick, flounce, and twirl. She closed her eyes—her elbows angling perilously toward the TV screen—and she imagined herself at a pep rally. Sixteen years old, no children to cart to school, shaggy-headed football players eyeing her knees.

As my mother danced, I wondered at this daring side of her. The year before, I'd gone to a birthday party and danced with some boys, my fingers clasped behind their sweaty necks. I'd confessed this sin to my mother, my voice faltering as I asked for absolution. And now my mother was dancing. Too shy to dance with her, I watched from a chair, imagining my skinny body in a kilt.

Shake Terribly the Earth

T HE SUMMER I WAS TWENTY-TWO, MY family drove six hours from Huntington, West Virginia, to an Indianapolis suburb to attend a funeral for Daniel, a man we barely knew. Three years earlier, in cold, windy January, we'd driven the same route for his wedding. Of course, we made both trips for his wife, my mom's fifty-something cousin Melody.

An ardent, divorce-hating Christian, Melody prayed for twenty years for her first husband to find God's grace and come back to her. Finally, she gave up, grew her thick blond hair to her shoulders, and smiled more. One summer at the Carter family reunion, Melody confided a secret to my mom over meatloaf. Her pastor had prophesied she'd meet someone soon. Six months later, my mom opened a wedding invitation with a snapshot: Melody, wrapped in the arms of a fit, handsome man in his late fifties with a full head of gray hair. My family almost never travels, but the fulfilled prophesy enraptured us. My mom started loading the minivan.

We barely made it to the wedding. With nearly an hour left of our directions, the van's digital clock displayed 1:00 pm, the time of the service. My dad bowed his head to the steering wheel. "I'm sorry, Marcy," he moaned to my mother. Then I remembered: there's an hour time difference between Huntington and Indianapolis. We pressed on.

We rolled onto the church parking lot at two minutes to one. My dad parked the van while the rest of us jogged in our dress shoes. Invitation in hand, we located the flower-choked chapel the card listed, and an usher directed us to chairs on the bride's side of the aisle. No one looked familiar. At first, we figured these strangers were Melody's friends from church, but we grew suspicious after a precious minute ticked by. Melody's sister Candy and their mother, my great-aunt Anita, should have been there. A man at the front with a groom-like grin had brown hair and a mustache. "Are you all here for Melody?" my mom asked the family beside us. No, they were not. They'd never heard of Melody. But there was another wedding in the sanctuary. Perhaps we might try that one? We ran again.

We knew we'd found the right place when Melody marched through a set of double doors in a tea-length cream dress. A clump of aunts and cousins welcomed us with a flurry of hugs as Melody hurried to the altar, laughing with joy.

✢ ✢ ✢

FOR the next three summers, we saw Melody and Daniel at the Carter reunion. They sat together in lawn chairs on Anita's sister Lita's back porch, sporting striped T-shirts and khaki shorts like a middle-aged Barbie and Ken. They held hands constantly; when a cousin separated them in the predinner prayer circle, Daniel protested, holding up the meal. Aunt Anita told me Daniel "scared the shit out" of her when she rode in his and Melody's backseat. He could spare only one hand for the steering wheel.

I smiled and talked to Melody, but I envied her. Before Melody met Daniel, I'd found her inspiring; she was sweet and funny, and she was single like me. Unpartnered in my midteens, I'd felt like a spinster. At Grace Christian School, the popular students had paired off in junior high and dated the same person through college. When they hit twenty-one, they sent their engagement notice to the local newspaper along with a picture: the boy in a tie, the girl in a blouse and lipstick. Next came the wedding picture, then biblical names in the births column. When I failed to snag a boyfriend in the seventh grade, I'd already fallen behind. At the reunion, I felt happy for Daniel and Melody when they flirted in the food line, but I found Melody's romance less comforting than her solitude.

My mom constantly assured me God was "saving me for someone special," but I was afraid she was wrong. I was painfully shy, and with my skinny body and my locker full of Jane Austen novels, all I'd attracted in high school was requests for algebra help. Once, a visiting minister preached a chapel sermon on navigating the gray areas between coal-black sex and shiny white occasional handholding. He chopped air with his hand, booming, "Should you draw the line here? or here? or here?" The couples squirmed. I didn't know what he was talking about. And my dearth of boyfriends hadn't improved since I'd started college, living at home and attending Marshall University.

A few boys did talk to me at Marshall, but I didn't waste my time talking back. I still loved Nick Joyce, now the front man for a local band called Fireproof. The band name advertised divine protection from the eternal fires of Hell. I became a groupie, just for the chance to see Nick. For two years after high school, I curled my hair and sang along at Fireproof gigs, held in parking lots, churches, and Christian coffeehouses. I bought band posters and waited in line to ask the musicians to autograph their own faces. When Nick held out his marker, I blushed and held my breath. "Thanks for coming out. Great to see you," he said. I took the opportunity to ogle his blue eyes.

At family reunions, I looked around at my generation of cousins, feeling inferior. They performed flips on the trampoline and lounged against the porch railing with cans of pop. Surely they'd all dated *someone*. Surely those cousins weren't waiting for years for their loves to notice their existence. Aunt Anita teased me: "Honey, you're holding out on me. I know you've got a boyfriend." Old uncles and middle-aged male cousins poked my dad and crowed, "I bet you have to beat the boys off her with a stick."

"Not yet," he answered. I wanted to crawl under the porch.

+ + +

A year after Melody's wedding, I had an epiphany at a Fireproof concert. In a cute T-shirt and thick mascara, I stood in a dim church sanctuary, jostling teenage girls for a prime spot by the altar. Nick, guitar in hand, grinned down from the pulpit's usual place. He preached a short sermon before his final song, assuring his fans that he and his bandmates—equipped with their big bass speakers, strobe lights, and flashy pyrotechnics—weren't the only ones who could win lost souls for the Lord. "Go on out there," he said, flashing his crooked smile, his neon highlights glowing orange. "The streets are your stage, and your words are your pyrotechnics." I groaned and stepped backward, letting a busty fan slide in front of me. What a clumsy, self-serving metaphor.

When the concert ended, I hung around out of habit, wondering if Nick would talk to me. He said a quick hello, asked me about college (he hadn't gone), and I drove home. That night, I lay in my bed in sleepless shock. Those orange highlights had really looked awful, and he'd gained thirty pounds since he quit playing high school sports. His songs seemed sincere, and he'd scored a recording contract from a Christian label in Nashville, but his lyrics had the literary merit of the *National Enquirer*. Suddenly, I could admit this. Even if he drove to my house and begged my forgiveness for all those wasted years, I no longer wanted *him*.

The morning after the concert, I filled the kitchen trash can with my Fireproof T-shirts, ticket stubs, and signed posters.

Then I found a pot of moldy spaghetti sauce in the refrigerator and drowned everything. I tore out every page of my journal that mentioned Nick and rinsed the crumpled paper in the bathroom sink until the words washed away. I remembered the prophecy of Isaiah: "When He ariseth to shake terribly the earth . . . a man shall cast his idols of silver, and his idols of gold . . . to the moles and to the bats." In an instant, my gold had become garbage.

✦ ✦ ✦

AND six months later, I found someone. It happened two weeks after my twenty-first birthday, two days after I'd spent another Valentine's Day eating chocolates with my mother. I felt ready to preach from the rooftops: when you let go, God can help you. Melody had prayed for her ex-husband for years, and when she'd given up, God had sent her Daniel. I gave up on Nick, and God had sent me someone too. I still believe in shedding useless obsessions, as long as you don't use your new freedom to plunge into something worse. Looking back, I can see omens of the coming disaster. He was only seventeen, his first name was Nick, and I decided I liked him before I met him.

My love story began when my sister Rebecca, a freshman at Spring Valley High School, met a cute blond senior named Todd Evicks. After I graduated from Grace Christian, my siblings had transferred to the Wayne County public school system, a land where boys wore camo pants and spat into pop bottles during class. Todd looked refreshingly shampooed and neat, and he loved books and the Newsboys, a Christian band my sisters and I had begun to adore after I trashed my Fireproof CDs. For months, Rebecca and Todd just e-mailed and passed notes by the lockers, but their hallway romance made me feel more spinsterly than ever. Even my little sister had a boyfriend.

Finally, Rebecca and Todd decided to meet away from school, at a foreign film. Todd's best friend Nick—another cute, blond senior—seemed to feel as left out as I did, and he acted excited when Rebecca told him about me: my 4.0 average, my passion for Chopin's nocturnes, my waist-length golden-brown hair. I had to drive Rebecca to the movie theater, so a double date was the best plan. I hesitated over Nick's age, and his first name made me queasy. But I did look young, especially without makeup. No one would realize I was a twenty-one-year-old dating a minor. And his last name made up for his unfortunate first: Darcy! I'd read *Pride and Prejudice* five times and watched the miniseries until I had it memorized. This had to be a sign from the Lord.

I hadn't been on a date since I met up with a boy at the mall bookstore in the sixth grade, telling my parents I planned to walk around "with friends," but I felt more than prepared. For years, I'd had a first date outfit planned, just in case; my most stylish pair of jeans and favorite shirt hung together in the back of my closet. When I bought a prettier blouse or a more chic pair of jeans, I updated my date outfit. Now *these* clothes would reel in a boy. I remember many hopeful ensembles: a sky-blue Adidas T-shirt and carpenter jeans, a floral blouse and a skort, a purple sweater and bell-bottoms. I can't remember that crucial outfit, the one I put on for a real date with Nick Darcy. Probably because he didn't show up.

Foreign films were a rarity in my town, so the theater was crowded. Long after the film began, I had to fight for my two empty aisle seats, turning away university professors and elderly couples in wool coats. When the film ended, I shivered outside the theater, watching for two boys, their faces pink from hurry and February cold. Rebecca watched with me, but she was more stoic; she'd see them at school the next day.

I had to give up. I got a sandwich with Rebecca and cried at the restaurant.

+ + +

A few years before Daniel met Melody, he discovered their future home in pieces down a long dirt road. A tornado had opened the bungalow like a dollhouse, and squirrels, mice, and birds were raising families in the rooms. Daniel bought the house without the property, and he trucked the halves across town and had them put back together next to the house where he grew up, where his elderly father still lived. Somehow, he added a basement with a secret room. He disguised the room's entrance—a sliding panel—with screwdrivers that dangled from hooks. In the room, he built intricate model airplanes and suspended them from the ceiling, in flight.

As a final decorative touch, Daniel added an accidental feline colony to his property. One day, he offered milk to a starving calico. Soon feral kittens sprawled in the flowerbeds while their parents hunted in the bushes.

I've heard two stories about how Daniel and Melody met. Aunt Anita told me the first story in Daniel and Melody's house, where close friends and relatives flocked to rest and chat after Daniel's viewing. The house hadn't yet realized that Daniel had died: his razor lay by the bathroom sink, and Melody's script on the kitchen wall calendar reminded him of next weekend's model airplane flying competition. A can of blue paint sat next to an unfinished model on Daniel's basement worktable, and, on the back wall of the garage—the first place Melody's eyes landed when she got home from work—Daniel's voice still echoed. One white letter on each red wooden heart: *I love you, Melody!*

In Aunt Anita's story, Melody and Daniel met in the late fall at the greenhouse where Daniel worked. A mutual friend had set them up, and they connected immediately. Daniel shyly clutched a pot of geraniums as Melody chattered and smiled, ignoring the cool wind that whipped her scarf tassels and pale wisps of hair around her blue eyes, fringed with tiny wrinkles but beautiful still. They exchanged phone numbers and addresses, and as soon as Melody got home, she sent a card: how lovely it was to meet him, and she'd like to see him again. Two weeks went by. Melody buried her hopes and prepared to forget him. Finally, Daniel called. The morning the card arrived, Daniel had contracted a terrible cold, and—Aunt Anita's words—he "couldn't be romantic when he was snotting all over the place." From then on, he visited Melody every evening, taking her out to fly model planes in the field behind his father's barn. "And six weeks later," Aunt Anita paused to chuckle, "wedding bells were ringing."

I heard the second story from Daniel's best friend, when he spoke at Daniel's funeral. In this story, Melody and Daniel met at the greenhouse, and Melody sent a card. But, this time, during those two weeks of silence, Daniel wasn't sick. After work in the evenings, he'd gone out as usual with his flying buddies. As tiny aircraft circled overhead, he'd spoken about Melody. He liked her, but he wasn't sure he ought to answer the card. "I'm happy as I am," Daniel had said, motioning toward the November-brown grass, the airplanes in the sky. "I don't think I'm ready for a relationship." The friend said he'd talked some sense into Daniel. Thirty years had passed since Daniel's divorce, and it wouldn't hurt to talk to this woman. "But," Daniel's friend added, looking sheepish, "I might have said something different if I'd known I'd see so little of my friend after that. He started spending all his time with Melody."

I prefer Aunt Anita's version, though the cold was probably an excuse. I don't like to picture Melody waiting, alone, with no answer on its way.

+ + +

AFTER the movie, Rebecca chided me as I moped over my sandwich. "Sarah Beth, stop it. You're acting like it's all over." And it wasn't over.

Nick found out my e-mail address, and when I got home, I discovered a message in my inbox. He'd been with Todd, Rebecca's failed date, at Todd's very pregnant aunt's birthday party. The boys had left the party early so they could meet us, but as Todd's car rolled down the driveway, Todd's uncle appeared, pushing his wife in front of him. She clutched her belly and wailed. Todd stopped, and the couple clambered into the backseat. "Hospital! Now!" the uncle screamed.

"We're going somewhere important. Could you take your car?" Nick pleaded.

"She's in labor!" the uncle snapped. "I'm not starting another car!"

By the time the boys had dropped off the couple, the movie had already started. "So, we went back to Todd's house and e-mailed you." Todd had written the same story to Rebecca, with fewer vivid details. Both boys begged, "Will you please forgive us?"

Of course I wrote back and forgave Nick. Their story seemed heroic, and a baby was involved. I worked in the church nursery, and I'd helped my mom diaper my younger siblings: I was a sucker for any story with a baby. In my e-mail, I asked Nick about his favorite Newsboys songs and his favorite books. When he was little, his mom had read him to sleep with Austen, and his middle name was Fitzwilliam. We wrote all afternoon. We discovered we had similar taste in everything: copper-nosed beagles, cherry cheesecake, Orczy's *Scarlet Pimpernel* series, the *Andy Griffith Show*. And the most crucial similarity: Nick was Pentecostal like me. Here was my chance to have a better marriage than my parents, to raise my happy, unconfused children to pray in tongues and dance in the Spirit.

That evening, I used my computer scanner to send Nick my high school senior picture. He wrote that he was even more excited to meet me after "suck a pretty picture." I cringed at the typo, but felt warm and happy anyway. Nick tried to e-mail a photo of himself, but he couldn't attach the file. Never mind, I told him. I'd see him soon. He lived less than a ten-minute drive from my house.

"Describe him to me," I asked Rebecca that night. I fell asleep happy, imagining Nick's navy-blue eyes, his jeans and white tennis shoes, the silky tufts that stuck out behind his ears.

+ + +

ALTHOUGH Nick Darcy lived less than a ten-minute drive away from me, I never met him. I like to believe if I'd seen his face and heard his voice, I wouldn't have fallen for him like I did.

Instead, for the next ten months, we wrote. Suddenly, I had an audience for the minute details of my day—the robin's nest by my window, a new pair of wool socks, an inspiring Bible verse from my daily devotions—that only someone who found me fascinating could enjoy. In person, he might have yawned and launched into a monologue about his rusty minivan, "the van of wonder." Safe behind my computer screen, I wrote my little narratives with perfect faith he reread them, searching for me in my writing the way I searched for him in his. Once, he wrote, "I'm going to print your e-mail and hug it."

He would have hugged me in person if he could, I was certain. Fate was conspiring against us. Days after the foreign film, Todd began vomiting every time he ate. Diagnosed with a rare blood disease, Todd had to drop out of high school, settling for a GED. Todd sent a few more e-mails to Rebecca, then he stopped. Nick e-mailed me almost daily, updating me on Todd's health, telling Rebecca that Todd missed her (she didn't believe it) and claiming he, Nick, was desperate to see me. Nick scheduled dates for the places couples from my high school had gone, Christian coffeehouses and Marshall University's Campus Christian Center, but he never appeared. Something new and horrible had happened to Todd—a hemorrhage, a fever of 105—and Nick had to stay with him.

When Nick didn't show up, I wept in public, wrinkling my ironed blouse and rinsing the curl from my hair, but I forgave him again. His sensational stories seduced me, and I admired his love for his friend. I remembered Fanny Price's fervent affection for her brother in *Mansfield Park*, love that inspired a passion in rakish Henry Crawford. Crawford wanted that love for himself. Armed with Austen, I believed Nick's love for Todd revealed how capable he was of loving me.

And Nick *did* love me. He told me he did within our first week of e-mails, and I took it as a good sign, not a warning. I'd waited three years for some sign of affection from Nick Joyce; I was ready for love to move quickly. Nick Darcy signed his first email "luv, Nick," a shy expression of interest. After I sent my picture, he signed off "luv ya." As our e-mail river deepened—my series of doomed hamsters, the early death of Nick's father from lung cancer, our confessions we'd both never been kissed—he signed "love ya," "love you," "I love you." I matched him exactly, believing we both wrote what we felt.

When disaster struck, and Nick couldn't see me, I was prepared to wait again, this time for a boy who loved me. My home and childhood church were filled with sojourners in the wilderness, wanderers just outside the Promised Land. My mom waited to escape her chronic illness and to buy a house with more than one bathroom. My mom's best friend waited for her teenage daughter to walk, speak, and think normally, free of the cerebral palsy that had struck her as a newborn. Members of New Life Victory Center waited for four-hundred-pound friends to grow thin, pot-smoking daughters to repent, gay sons to marry women. Like Hannah in the Bible, they clung to temple pillars and sobbed, praying for life in their barren wombs. Like David, they hid like madmen in caves, believing one day they'd be king.

I trudged through my wilderness, writing my love daily and reading Psalm 126 every night. "When the LORD turned again the captivity of Zion, we were like them that dream." In *my* dream, Nick Darcy took walks in the woods with my old beagle and me. We searched for birds' nests and kissed in the bushes. I prayed, "Turn again our captivity, O LORD, as the streams in the south."

✦ ✦ ✦

IN my wilderness fervor, I ignored the signs that should have told me the whole thing was a scam. Nick never remembered to give me his address, and he refused to give me a phone number. A ringing phone might wake Todd; it would be best if Nick called *me*. I gave him my phone number again when he lost it under his bed, and I shooed my parents and siblings off the dial-up Internet every night for the next week. Still, Nick insisted my line was always busy. "I guess something's wrong with my phone," he wrote. I found this lame, but let it pass. I believed in Nick in the same way I believed in the Bible at that time: with a fierce, frightened determination. If Jacob's twin brother Esau wasn't born with fuzzy red hair on his tiny chest and limbs, could I believe a God existed who loved me? And if Nick had never tried to call me at all—I couldn't imagine the alternative. It was safest to question nothing.

Increasingly desperate to see and touch Nick, I haunted the places he mentioned in his e-mails. A grocery store, McDonald's, the tutoring center at his high school. I talked my family into visiting Jefferson Avenue Church of God, the church Nick and Todd claimed to attend. He wasn't there, and no one had heard of either the Darcy or the Evicks family. But I figured the Evickses and Darcys had neglected church after Todd got so sick, and surely two families could be forgotten in a congregation of five hundred people.

Nick told me he wrote his e-mails from the local library, so I showed up every afternoon, breathlessly checking the aisles and computers, peering hopefully at the closed men's room door. The librarian must have thought I was a nut. Whenever Todd had an emergency, I called all three hospitals and asked for his room number, but the nurses told me Todd wasn't there. In my frantic search, I purposely overlooked a crucial detail: even if I'd found Nick, I couldn't have been sure it was him. He'd never sent a picture, and I couldn't find him in the high school yearbooks. Some disaster had always happened on picture day. I had to imagine a face for my beloved.

My family didn't understand. My dad had watched *Pride and Prejudice* along with me, and he borrowed, too appropriately, from sarcastic Mr. Bennet's critique of the villainous liar George Wickham. Imitating Mr. Bennet's British accent, he declared, "With such narratives at hand, who would read novels?" Like Elizabeth Bennet, I defended my man with righteous anger, but secretly I feared my dad was right. I'd collected Nick's e-mails in a binder and read them like my own epistolary novel, savoring the developing story.

My mother had encouraged my long-suffering love for singer Nick, but this Nick worried her. Once she called him my "invisible boyfriend," and I hurled my shoe at her. Only Rebecca comforted me, reciting every word Nick had said in the hallway, describing the rubber pickle he kept in his locker. She seemed to believe in him, but she told me, years later, she'd felt guilty for leading me into that mess.

As the months passed, I began to dread the Carter reunion. I'd hoped Nick would show up and come with me, proving to my relatives there was at least one boy for my dad to beat away with a stick. But Nick's plot had complicated further: his flighty, gorgeous mother had vanished for weeks, leaving her son and twin seven-year-old daughters with Todd's family. Nick had to watch his sisters every evening; he couldn't possibly ask Todd's parents to babysit.

Then, one day, Rebecca found tangible hope in the drainage ditch behind our mailbox. A soggy, torn graduation announcement for Nicholas Fitzwilliam Darcy. He'd tucked a letter for me inside the card. A real paper letter and an invitation to his graduation, a place he'd definitely be! Nick had scrawled the wrong house number on the envelope, so I figured a neighbor had attached the letter to the outside of our mailbox, and wind or a dog had carried it away.

Mud had soaked away most of the return address, but I put on extra mascara and drove to the street the envelope seemed to indicate. I felt nervous when I approached even my relatives' closed doors, and Todd's street, where Nick was staying, had three-story homes with skylights, real wood siding, and chemical-green lawns swept clean of sticks and leaves. In my neighborhood, loose mutts trotted past ranchers with particleboard or vinyl siding, and baseball mitts and turtle-shaped sandboxes nestled in overgrown front yards. But my determination gave me courage. I rang every doorbell on the street, asking for the Evicks family. Busy moms, impatient men in suits, and elderly men in plush robes answered the doors. Again and again: "Hmm. Never heard of them. Maybe they live somewhere further down the road." I went home tired and humiliated. "It's my fault," I told my mom and Rebecca. "I must have picked the wrong street."

Still, I refused to despair. I had a letter now, not an e-mail, something Nick had actually touched. After I had the letter memorized, I placed it in a cardboard necklace box along with the announcement and muddy envelope, inking "Most Precious Treasures" on the box lid. Without a touch of irony, I imitated naïve Harriet Smith of Austen's *Emma,* a girl who boxed and cherished her own "Most Precious Treasures": a broken pencil and a bandage that had once held the warmth of her coldhearted beloved's hands. I kept my treasures by my bed when I slept.

The day of the graduation came, and I got up early to paint my toenails and iron my best date outfit yet: pale blue blouse, off-white skirt with tiny red and blue daisies. The colors coordinated with the bright balloon-print wrapping paper on Nick's graduation gift. I planned to arrive an hour before the ceremony and search until I found my beloved. I pictured myself pinning on Nick's graduation cap, resting my fingers in his hair.

On the way out the door, I checked my e-mail and found a message from Todd. Nick's mother had returned that morning, married and pregnant with a new set of twins. Her new husband was wealthy but brutal, and she needed Nick and her girls to move to Nashville with her that night. "Nick would have e-mailed you himself," Todd wrote, "but he can't stop puking. He wanted to see you more than anything." I lay on my bedroom floor in my date outfit, feeling that life was too much to bear.

In June, I faced the reunion bravely, sleeping in a tent with my siblings and cousins in my great-aunt Lita's backyard, smiling at Daniel and Melody when they chatted about their hiking trips. But I noticed some relatives staring at me, and I heard my name whispered around the patio table as I walked by.

I cornered my mother in the bathroom and demanded the truth. Aunt Lita had telephoned before the reunion, and my mom had told her about Nick. My moping had frustrated my mom, and it was a good story to tell on the phone. Aunt Lita had told everyone, probably (and justly) asking them to pray for me. That year was low on spicy family news—no fresh teen pregnancies, divorces, or tattoos—so a niece with a boyfriend she'd never met seemed deliciously gossip-worthy. I took refuge on the swing next to Aunt Anita, hoping to hear some old stories as I ate my casserole. I shouldn't have trusted her. Still lovely in her eighties, with five divorces behind her, Aunt Anita felt uniquely equipped to give advice about men.

Aunt Anita yarned for a while, telling me about the time she'd dyed her hair green during World War II rationing, and she'd had to wait a year to dye her hair blond again. Waitressing at a diner, she'd pretended her head scarf was a fashion statement. Then Aunt Anita put her hand on my knee. "Sarah Beth," she said, her voice a very audible whisper, "I've heard about your little boyfriend, and you need to get rid of him. We've got enough weirdos in this family." I laughed, but I wanted to cry.

+ + +

I was devastated when Nick moved away, but I was also relieved. I told new friends about my long-distance boyfriend in Tennessee; now there was a reason we were apart.

I asked Nick for an address so I could write letters, and to my happy surprise, he gave me one. I was excited about letter writing, sending my love something he could touch and keep, maybe in a special box like mine. But I really wanted the address so I could visit him. I'd never driven longer than an hour in my life, but *this* was a time for travel.

Nick begged me not to come—his stepfather was evil and his mother was ill—but if I drove 350 miles alone, surely no one would turn me away. I plugged the address into MapQuest, and the program couldn't locate it. I e-mailed Nick to check the house number and zip code, and he assured me everything was correct. I gave up for the moment and comforted myself with letter writing, mailing a fat envelope every few days. I wished for a letter in return, so I read by the window every morning until I saw the mailman's turquoise Jeep. Nothing came. After a couple of weeks, the Jeep delivered my own letters; a menacing red finger framed the words "Return to Sender." Nick quickly figured it out. His stepfather didn't want him or his mother to receive mail, so he'd bought a rubber stamp and sent everything back. "Try again," Nick e-mailed. "I'll beat him to the mailbox." I sent another volley of letters, and again they came back. I kept writing letters and stashed them in my closet, waiting for better times.

Nick's last e-mail came in early December: a short declaration of his helplessness and undying love. Of course he didn't tell me I'd never hear from him again. By this time, I understood I wouldn't see him at Christmas, but I bought him a sweater anyway. I sulked in a recliner while my siblings hung candy canes from the tree.

The next semester, I ignored my empty inbox and threw myself into my schoolwork. I was trying to put off grieving. Researching Victorian governesses, I studied 150-year-old diaries and issue after issue of *The Times*, burning my fingers on flapping microfilm when I loaded the reader incorrectly. Teaching, mending, diapering for £10 a year: the governesses' lives were rougher than mine.

I still e-mailed Nick, but I stopped narrating my day and started telling him what a loser he was. I reminded him of Frank Churchill in *Emma*, how he claimed his aunt was ill when he didn't care to visit his father. I accused Nick of Bunburying. Nick no longer bothered to send his excuses, but I wanted him to know I suspected them.

On a whim, I researched Nick's Nashville address again, and I found he'd given me a zip code that didn't exist. I couldn't lie to myself after that. In April, I wrote him a final time, telling him I knew he'd lied about the zip code and "probably a lot of other things, too." I assured him I would find someone better, though I didn't believe it. I still cherished my imaginary lover: shaggy blond hair, clean tennis shoes, his slender body in a red cotton T-shirt. I figured he'd grow up and marry some girl, and I still wanted that girl to be me.

When school ended in May, I devoted myself to despair. I experienced Nick's betrayal as a physical pain in my chest, so intense I looked for a wound. At night, Rebecca lay on a pile of sleeping bags and pillows next to my twin bed so I wouldn't sob instead of sleep. My self-esteem plummeted. I survived on oatmeal raisin cookies and dropped to a skeletal 103. "You're so thin!" my boss told me at work. I couldn't tell if she was envious or worried.

I reread Austen's *Sense and Sensibility* and wept along with the heartbroken sisters. I understood, too well, Marianne's quest for her runaway lover: her desperate journey to London; her endless stream of tearstained letters; her days of waiting at home by the window, every muscle strained for a visit, or at least a note. Months later, Willoughby admitted how carefully he'd avoided Marianne. He'd ducked into shops and escaped from balls, afraid she would scream at him or hurl herself into his arms. I wondered if Nick had spent the year fleeing from gas stations when he heard Rebecca's voice, hiding behind Coca-Cola displays when he saw a skinny girl with my waist-length golden-brown hair.

Willoughby told Marianne's sister, "There was hardly a day in which I did not catch a glimpse of one or other of you; and nothing but the most constant watchfulness on my side . . . could have separated us so long."

+ + +

UNLIKE most online stalkers, Nick had posed no sexual threat, but I felt ugly instead of thankful. Irrationally, I thought I might have recovered more easily if Nick *had* been a sexual predator; at least then I would have known why he was interested. If he didn't want to touch me, why had he bothered with me at all?

I flattered myself he'd enjoyed my ruminations about Chopin, my stories about the tadpoles in our inflatable pool. But then, why didn't he come over to hear a nocturne, or to see the tadpoles' newly sprouted legs for himself? Why would he bother to write me dozens of e-mails if he didn't care to sneak a kiss behind the apple tree? I felt cheated: all that grief and I'd still never been kissed. I had no right to feel righteous about my perfect virginity. I'd never been tempted to give it away.

Now, seven years later, I realize Nick and I likely had very little in common. He probably looked online for obscure quotes from *Pride and Prejudice* and read Rebecca's e-mails to Todd, skimming for songs and movies he could name-drop to me. It was easy enough to claim he was Pentecostal and find a

Pentecostal church in the Huntington phone book. Rebecca learned later through some sleuthing at Spring Valley High School that Todd had signed a fake last name on the first note he passed her in the hallway. His real name was Adkins. No wonder I couldn't find the Evicks family. Nick's more improbable last name seems to have been real, far too perfect to change.

A year after the Nick disaster, I wrote a story for a fiction class about a naïve girl who gets duped by a boy through a year-long series of e-mails. When my classmates told me the story was implausible, I admitted, blushing with pride and humiliation, that I'd taken the story from personal experience. A boy in my class laughed nervously and said, "Wow, I feel bad now." He'd attended Spring Valley High School, one class ahead of Nick and Todd. He'd never met my invisible boyfriend, but he and his friends had had some fun lying to girls through e-mail. "But I didn't do it for that long," he said. "That's crazy!"

It is crazy. It made me feel slightly better, or angrier, to learn other girls had been through the same thing, but the length of time sets my situation apart from the practical jokes my class-mate admitted to pulling. A jokester laughs as his victim falls in the mud, tells the story until it mildews, then looks for some-one else to dupe. Nick's e-mailed saga is more like the work of a con man, a seductive stranger who'd eventually disappear, with my heirloom jewelry rattling in the trunk of his car. I think Nick enjoyed the con—my earnest professions of love, my abso-lute faith in his wild stories—and his vanishing act was all the more dramatic since he'd never appeared in the first place. But other than my innocence, I didn't seem to have anything he wanted to steal.

I wonder now if Nick and Todd were in love with each other, and Nick strung me along for safety, in case he needed to produce a girlfriend at a family reunion of his own. South-ern West Virginia isn't the happiest place to be gay. Nick was certainly closer to Todd than he wanted to be to me, and

Rebecca told me Nick and Todd sometimes wore their hair in pigtails and painted their nails. They blamed the purple nails on Todd's little sister and explained the hair by boasting they weren't "restricted by gender." At the time, I found this progressive and cute.

Or maybe Nick wasn't gay at all, but just your average sociopath, e-mailing ten other girls along with me. By now, he might have six wives in three states. Really, I suppose I'm thankful, or ought to be. I didn't get date-raped or left for dead in an alley. I didn't end up jobless and pregnant, or racked with an STD. But at twenty-two, I couldn't feel anything but bereft.

+ + +

IN midsummer, my despair hit its peak, and my mom dragged me to the Carter reunion. Aunt Anita told me, "Honey, I heard it was all over with that boy. I'm so happy."

Daniel and Melody were past the matching stage, but they held hands as they sipped their bottled water and refused dessert. Hip. Healthy. Middle-aged trendy. Everyone else held a beer or a can of pop. I had no idea Daniel was watching what he ate because of his heart condition. After dinner, Daniel whipped out a video camera and recorded only Melody. Melody stroking a child's hair, Melody petting a cousin's dog, Melody laughing with her mother on the swing.

Two months later, we got a call from Aunt Lita. Daniel had died of a heart attack. My mom started loading the minivan.

+ + +

ON Daniel's last day, he and Melody had planned to go on a picnic with a church group. As Melody buttoned her blouse, Daniel appeared in the bathroom. "Let's not go," he urged. "I want to spend time with you."

Hand in hand, they wandered over Daniel's father's property, stooping to pet a tiger-striped kitten, pausing to kiss in the barn that housed a pack of cats and a fifty-year-old Ford. The couple walked a mile through the woods to the airfield Daniel and his brother, both pilots, had built together in their twenties. The family had long since sold the field to the state, and Daniel contented himself now with his models. A Cessna took off and Melody imagined a young Daniel, with brown hair. Young Daniel soared away from Indianapolis, looking down at the Indiana cornfields.

They walked back to the house and made love; afternoon sunlight bathed them through the blinds. When they'd finished, Daniel's body stiffened on top of Melody's, his face blank. Melody screamed, *Jesus.* Daniel had died immediately. Melody shoved him off her and called the ambulance and prayed on the bed until she heard the siren.

+ + +

WHEN my family arrived at the viewing, Melody's sister Candy couldn't resist. She took my mother's hand and narrowed her eyes. "Are you sure you're at the right funeral?"

We were at the right funeral. We'd double-checked the white letters on the black velvet sign on the way into the funeral home. Still, I felt disconcerted. If the casket and flower baskets hadn't leered from the corner, I could have sworn we'd wandered into a wedding anniversary celebration by mistake. Three days before, Daniel had been alive, fifty-nine years old, joyously married to Melody. No one seemed ready to forget this.

Melody had replaced the funeral home's mournful background music with a medley of her and Daniel's favorite upbeat Christian songs. Friends gossiped and joked. Relatives munched on homemade cakes in an adjoining room. On a screen near the casket, photos flashed: tiny barefoot Daniel with his brothers, young Daniel grinning beside the wing of a small airplane, gray-haired Daniel hugging a rescued raccoon, hugging Melody. Then, tiny Melody with colorized yellow pigtails, teenage Melody in a yearbook, grown-up Melody in Daniel's arms. Real Melody greeted guests by the casket with a bright, shaky smile.

A church friend remarked, "Melody's doing so well!"

Candy's husband muttered, "She's doing well now." His tone drew a picture: Melody sobbing on the floor.

The funeral the next day had the same aura of forced happiness. The service focused on the marriage, not the death. Daniel's best friend told his story about the day the couple met. Melody took the pulpit and preached patience and forgiveness, assuring the unconvinced audience her marriage had been as imperfect as theirs. Melody had our attention; before she began speaking, she'd turned to the still-open casket and smiled. "Isn't it wonderful, Darling, that all these people came to see us?" I can't imagine how she felt when the funeral director closed the lid.

✢ ✢ ✢

WHEN I arrived at Daniel's funeral, I still envied Melody. For three years, she'd been gloriously happy. She'd eaten with Daniel, made love with Daniel, watched as he built his airplanes. She'd known his family, and he'd known hers. If Nick had died and I'd gone to his funeral, no one would have known who I was. But when I witnessed Melody's strength, I also felt ashamed of myself, and I realized I was going to be okay.

And I am okay. I'm tempted to scoff at my trivial young heartbreak, especially when I think about Melody's authentic tragedy. Nick Darcy was just a teenager who lied to me on the Internet.

But even though my boyfriend was imaginary, my pain wasn't, and neither was the anguish I felt as a kindergartner, abandoned on a seesaw by my onetime best friend. In *Middlemarch*, one of my favorite Victorian novels, George Eliot defends the moping young. She asks readers to sympathize with her young characters, all of them fraught with despair. "If youth is the season of hope," she writes, "it is often so only in the sense that our elders are hopeful about us. . . . Each crisis seems final, simply because it is new. . . . The oldest inhabitants in Peru do not cease to be agitated by earthquakes, but they probably see beyond each shock, and reflect that there are plenty more to come." When Daniel died, Melody's first husband had already cheated on her. She'd raised her daughters by herself and survived two decades alone. Melody's mother was in her eighties; Anita couldn't live forever. Melody's earth had quaked before, and it would certainly quake again. At fifty-four, Melody could see this. At twenty-two, I could not.

And I learned something on that trip to Indiana. Different as we were in life experience and maturity, Melody and I shared a secret bane: the reunions. All that anxious, gossipy love. At dinner after the funeral, Melody spoke to my mother and me alone for a few minutes. With tearful relief, she told us she didn't need to marry again. "I'm a completed woman. Now every year at the reunion people won't look at me and think, There's Melody alone. They'll think, There's Melody, and she lost her Daniel."

+ + +

AFTER Daniel's funeral, I began to heal, and to heal I had to throw things away. When I got over my first Nick, I cast my keepsakes "to the moles and to the bats" without regret. But this time, my earth had shaken more terribly than before, and so, the purging was a process.

For a boy I never saw, I'd amassed an impressive stash of keepsakes. Printed e-mails. Electronic e-mails. Boxes of my own letters. CDs I'd bought him. His Christmas sweater. His graduation gift, a T-shirt that claimed its wearer had been *Saved by the Scarlet Pimpernel*. A fuzzy candid I'd cut from a yearbook in hopes that the possibly blond boy might be him. Every few weeks, I found the courage to get rid of a few items. I threw out the paper e-mails, and, later, I deleted all of the files. Last of all, I smashed my Most Precious Treasures box and shredded the muddy scraps of paper. I found new inspiration in *Emma's* Harriet Smith: she dropped her Treasures into the fireplace after her beloved married someone else.

Melody emptied her life out too. After Daniel's funeral, she moved to Arizona. Her daughters lived there, and she couldn't handle living in Daniel's house, sleeping in Daniel's bed, going to the same grocery store and dry cleaners she'd used when she'd been so happy. Melody sought a new landscape, trading the flat suburbs and cornfields for the desert. Aunt Anita went with her and stayed for a year; she knew her daughter needed her.

But before Melody left, she had to clean out the house. Daniel was gone, and she couldn't haul his nearly sixty years of mementos across the country. She donated what she could, sending Daniel's shirts and suits to the Goodwill, his model planes to a local museum. She divided the photo albums with Daniel's father. Daniel's razor, socks, and toothbrush—the relics of his daily life—she had to throw away.

And she had to get rid of the cats. The house was for sale, and few prospective buyers would jump for a place that came with forty-five felines.

"You have to quit feeding them," a friend told her.

"I can't," Melody insisted, but she did. Day after day, cats meowed on the back porch, hungry. Melody closed the blinds and hugged her housecat, feeling treacherous. After a week, only a few determined calicos scratched at the door, and after two weeks, the last cat slunk away.

Melody scrubbed paw prints from the cobblestones and raked fur and feces from the flower gardens until every trace of cat disappeared.

November Leaves

WHEN THE SKY IS CLOUDLESS AND MY parents are happy, my mother tells the story of her wedding day. "Usually it's cloudy in November, but the sky looked just like this," she sighs. She stares through the glass back door at the cobalt patches between the trees. In the West Virginia November, shriveled leaf scraps cling to naked branches, but that year must have been different. No rainstorms, perhaps. A scarlet-clothed dogwood glowed against the white Methodist church as Marcy and David descended the front steps, hand in hand.

"God gave us a perfect day," she tells me. "It was so warm I didn't have to put a coat over the dress Grandma made for my honeymoon. That was my *real* wedding dress, not my cheap, ugly wedding gown." I have the honeymoon dress in my closet now: a knee-length polyester print of rust, cerulean, and gold, trimmed with navy rickrack. The colors must have outshone the leaves.

In that dress, Marcy hurried across the church parking lot, skirt and brown curls flapping behind her, and she climbed into the passenger seat of a blue Ford sedan. David slid in beside her and shyly squeezed her knee. Marcy smiled and waved at some friends on the church steps; she didn't know they'd poured rice into her suitcase. Then off the couple drove into the future.

But when rain pounds the back porch and my parents aren't speaking, my mother tells a different story. This version emerges after long, lonely weeks: the same program droning on both TVs; cats curled on David's side of the bed; a droop in David's neck from the family room futon. Every night, he stakes his claim with a pillow so his wife will take the bed. He knows her back can't handle a thin mattress.

In this other story, my mother wore her beloved dress, but she plodded toward the sedan. She stopped a few car-lengths short and made sure the rice-pourers were out of earshot.

"You know, we haven't consummated this marriage yet," she whispered. "We can still get it annulled."

David's eyes blazed and his jaw tightened. He jerked his new wife's arm toward the car and growled, "Come on." Off they drove to the motel, leaving youth and virginity behind them.

I can't reconcile these two stories. I can't believe my mother could say such a thing on that warm, cloudless day. Or that my father responded so brutally in the shade of that scarlet dogwood. When my mother tells the second story, I reimagine the setting: gray sky, bare branches, damp flakes of early snow.

✦ ✦ ✦

AS always, the truth must lie outside these conflicting versions. To seek the true, true story of my parents as they left that Methodist church, I'd also need to ask my father, an eavesdropping wedding guest, and a robin, long dead by now, who listened from the lowest branch of the dogwood tree.

But I'm not sure these extra versions would bring clarity. My dad would tell me what he remembered, but he would filter his details through the sieve of his current day: the color of the sky, the snarls he had faced at work, the last conversation he'd had with my mother. And my dad's degree of happiness, or frustration, during the storytelling moment might determine how much he would allow me, his daughter, to hear.

My family communicates in stories. To say she loves me, my mom has told me I was the most beautiful newborn in the hospital nursery; Ralph gloated as strangers admired his new grandbaby through the glass. To tell me I'm whiny and ungrateful, my mom has spun yarns that made my problems look small: the days she sat, cold and hungry, on concrete steps, counting pennies to buy cigarettes for her mother. I can spot a brewing storm between my parents, miles in the distance, by the wedding day story my mother tells. The rest of my family is the same: grandparents, aunts, uncles, cousins yarn about the Great Depression, switch-wielding math teachers, communists posing as harmless radio hosts, nickels on dead people's eyes. The same stories, again and again, never quite the same, all tainted by faulty memory, by imagination, by sunshine, by mood.

I sit and listen, like the robin in the dogwood, gleaning nuances from each telling of each story. Each self-contradicting version builds a broader space where the truth can reside, but the truer truth lies in the telling. When my mother tells a version of her wedding day story, the tale gives me a window into my mother's life. I learn how she feels, and who she is, at that moment. And through the versions of my family's stories I choose to capture or amalgamate, I reveal the same things about myself.

Boat Stories: Three Generations

ne

During a thunderstorm in the South Pacific, an enormous green tail washed over the prow of a ship. World War II was winding down, and Elwood Childers was serving in the navy. He was eighteen. For hours, waves had rocked the cruiser like a bathtub sailboat, the ends of the ship alternately pointing toward the storm-black ocean and the dark clouds and pelting rain. A wall of water hit the ship, and the prow plunged deep into the sea—the sailors clung by their fingernails to the paint on the deck railings—and then the prow sprang back up, the tail coming with it, muscle glistening under skin in the bursts of lightning. Elwood saw only a tail, not the creature that owned it: waves concealed both the tail's base and tip. Moments later, the boat dipped again, and the tail slipped back into the waves.

When my siblings and I were little, Grandpa told us this story many times. Sitting in the lamplight at his particleboard dining room table, he leaned over his cup of coffee, his blue eyes round, and we forgot all about our graham crackers and milk. I imagined the slippery creature lurking, even as he spoke, in an underwater lair, surrounded by the bones of whales, its prey.

When we'd had our fill of the storm story, Grandpa yarned about his childhood on a small West Virginia farm: about the day he got lost as a six-year-old on his solitary walk to the one-room schoolhouse, and about his scruffy cat Old Tom who decided to live wild on the chipmunks and voles he caught in the woods. And he told us other tales from his years in the navy: the shark he nearly stepped on while swimming off the coast of Australia; the cook who sliced off his own index finger, hoping to be sent home; the domesticated duck that sneaked on board in the Philippines only to abandon ship far from freshwater and land, a forlorn white speck bobbing on the waves. I listened transfixed to all Grandpa's stories, wishing I could live on a farm, befriending the foals and chickens, or travel the world's seas on a ship, keeping my balance on the rocking deck, but the story of the sea creature stood out from the rest. Only this story expanded my ideas of the possible, and only this story required an illustration. Whenever Grandpa told about the tail, he took a blue ink pen from the pocket of his short-sleeved cotton shirt and drew a diagram on the pastel notepaper MaMa kept by the phone. First he sketched the front half of the tilting ship, then he colored in the tail that weighed the vessel down, his pen nib carving into the thick pink paper.

At the end of the story, after the tail disappeared, the sailors stared at the foaming, empty sea in disbelief, hoping a massive body would surface. They ignored for the moment the storm that had stolen their white hats and drenched the blue jeans they'd softened by dragging them behind the ship on a rope. "Did you see that?" Elwood and the other sailors asked, looking into each other's frantic eyes for affirmation. Their curses and answers confirmed it: Yes, they'd seen it. The tail was real. When Grandpa told me the story, the sailors' answers verified the existence of that tail for me. I was certain the appendage belonged to an ocean-dwelling dinosaur, a blood relation to the Loch Ness monster, stirred by the tempest from its hiding place on the ocean floor.

Years later, when I was in college, I heard my dad's older brother Mike chuckle at his father's stories, told that winter over Christmas dinner. He pointed out the ridiculousness of the giant tail and the unlikelihood that a loose duck would stow away and live willingly on board with the sailors for weeks, as Grandpa claimed. "There's no way that stuff's true," Mike said, to a clutch of us eating pumpkin pie at a card table set up by the stove. "Well, *some* of it's true, but those stories have grown over the years." I was horrified. Grandpa was eating his pie in the next room, at that table where he'd always told his stories, and I leaned back in my chair to look through the doorway, to make sure he was still happily yarning, oblivious. I remained silent, unsure what to say, unwilling to ask my uncle if his father's tales had changed since Mike was a little boy. I realized I'd always believed everything Grandpa had told us with an almost religious fervor; it had never occurred to me to view the great adventurer as a retired warehouse manager exaggerating the experiences of his youth. I knew my mother believed the stories—considered the creature's tail a proof of Creationism—and my dad had never disputed the stories' truth on the car rides home. I found it safe, comforting, to keep on believing. If I questioned the truth of Grandpa's stories, I'd have to doubt Mike's and my dad's stories, even my mom's, even my own.

But after Uncle Mike laughed at Grandpa, I did question the tail story. I still believed my grandpa saw *something*, but I started coming up with my own theories about what it might have been. I wanted to believe the story, but I wanted to base my belief on logic and science. So, I thought, maybe it wasn't a dinosaur tail after all. Maybe it was part of a giant squid. I'd read about them in *Moby Dick*, a waterlogged tale of ocean adventure I'd enjoyed all the more because I loved Grandpa's stories. In the novel, the whalers see a giant squid as they sail the Indian Ocean, up the coast of Australia toward Java (the opposite side of Australia from where Grandpa almost stepped on a shark). One "transparent blue" morning, a glorious white cloud floats before the ship on the water. Ishmael describes the creature as "the most wondrous phenomenon which the secret seas have hitherto revealed to mankind. A vast pulpy mass, furlongs in length and breadth, of a glancing cream-color, lay floating on the water, innumerable long arms radiating from its centre, and curling and twisting like a nest of anacondas, as if blindly to clutch at any hapless object within reach. . . . It . . . undulated there on the billows, an unearthly, formless, chance-like apparition of life."

After the squid disappears, sinking back into the ocean with a "low sucking sound," Ishmael's superstitious fellow sailors grip the sides of the ship in horror, stricken at the sight of the ominous "white ghost." They don't treasure up this rare sighting, jot it on limp notepaper to send home to their sweethearts, or commit it to memory to share with their grandchildren. Now that they've seen the squid, they're certain they'll never return home at all. Ishmael, however, seems to revel in the memory as he narrates the story for us, his readers, the way Grandpa did when he described that mysterious thing that washed onto his ship in the storm.

Reading Ishmael's description now, years later, I'm not sure why I thought Grandpa's tail could have been a squid, a white "pulpy mass" like a "nest of anacondas," though Grandpa might have mistaken the creature's color through the rain. Perhaps several tentacles might have draped across the ship's prow at once, but that's not what Grandpa said he saw. The only real similarity between the stories is that Ishmael and Grandpa both saw something wondrous rare, something only those who go to sea ever have a chance to witness.

I'm content now that I don't know the truth of Grandpa's story: if what washed up on Grandpa's ship was a massive tail, squid tentacles, a tangled clump of seaweed, or nothing at all. I don't need to question the details. The stories themselves are what's important. In Grandpa's story, in his memory, a tail washed up on a ship. To me, the faraway South Pacific in Grandpa's stories is like the otherworld in medieval romances, the sea in *Moby Dick*—a place where anything might happen.

Two

Growing up, Elwood's sons lived less than a block from the Ohio River. In the summers, David and Mike placed fat slices of bologna on the back porch in the sun, out of the reach of neighborhood dogs, until the meat toughened, shrank, and curled, perfect for clinging to a fishhook. The boys got up at five the next morning, grabbed their bait and fishing poles, and opened the backyard pen so their beagle could trot on ahead of them to the floodwall.

In other parts of Huntington, the floodwall is made of ugly brown concrete, but in David and Mike's childhood neighborhood, it's a grass-covered manmade hill. On top, the wall is flat and ten feet wide, perfect for jogging or for boarding a sled. The wall's sides slope downward at forty-five degree angles: steep enough for a good whoosh on a sled, but not too steep for little David to race up and down, catching crickets in the purple deadnettle. On their early fishing mornings, the brothers and the beagle climbed over the floodwall and headed through a strip of ivy and silver maples to the riverbank. As the sun crept up around a bend in the Ohio River, David used the bologna to catch minnows that Mike loaded onto his own hook in pursuit of the real prey: catfish.

As the brothers sat on the bank, digging their bare toes into the mud, waiting for a tug on their line, they watched boats glide down the river, on out of sight. Quiet rowboats kept to the shady edges, fishing lines trailing behind them, and motorboats sped down the middle, their decks covered with teenagers who stretched their tanned legs in the sun. Big white barges, miniature ships, pushed their broad sheets of coal, sounding their horns to warn the smaller boats to get out of the way. The barge workers in their hats and sweaty T-shirts shouted happily to each other, forgetting the danger of their work. Some of the middle-aged bargemen might have imagined themselves still young and at war, steaming past the Philippines instead of between the banks of the Ohio.

Watching the water traffic pass them by, Mike and David started wishing *they* had a boat. They wanted to float midriver and cast their lines down to where they figured the biggest fish hid. They wanted to go somewhere, to cross the invisible state line and stand on the opposite bank, in Ohio. And they wanted to escape from the land, to rock on the current.

The boys spotted it one morning as they sat on the riverbank with their fishing poles, cooling their feet in the muddy water. An iron, square-bottomed rowboat had settled into the pebbles in the shallows by the bank, its hull collecting cardboard milk cartons, tin bait cans, shiny black mussels, and leaves. Completely submerged, the little vessel bore the story of someone else's boating disaster. But it was a boat. Uncle Mike's eyes light up over his gray beard as he tells the story. "It was amazing. About the best thing we could find. A boat!" At that time, Mike was only two years younger than Grandpa had been when he joined the navy on his seventeenth birthday. David was ten.

Mike and David reeled in their lines and dropped their poles on the bank—catfish were boring now—and together they dragged the boat out of the river, tipping it up to drain the water and debris. "I don't know how we ever got it out of the water!" my dad says now, marveling. "That thing was made of *iron*. It must have weighed hundreds of pounds. It wasn't light like our aluminum canoe." I've never thought of our canoe as light: I groan after Saturday canoe trips when I have to help my dad and sisters hoist the thing back on top of the minivan. I picture the two boys lifting that iron boat, determined in spite of its weight. Their faces strain beneath their summer buzz cuts; river water streaks their T-shirts with mud and algae as they lug their prize onto the riverbank.

After that hunk of iron sat dripping into the tall grass and mud, the boys realized it would be impossible to shoulder it home to fix it. So, they took their fishing poles back to Grandpa's backyard storage building and grabbed the Radio Flyer wagon they kept for riding down the floodwall into the neighborhood, steering with the handle away from trees, houses, parked cars, and the ceramic frogs on the lawns. They ran with their wagon back to the river, where they balanced the boat on top of the toy's frame. The thin red steel bent and bowed under the weight. Then the boys inched back through the silver maples to the floodwall; David tugged the handle in front and Mike guided from behind.

The floodwall posed the biggest challenge. The boys couldn't risk letting the boat roll down the hill into the river on the one side or into a neighbor's child, cat, or car on the other, so they had to dump the boat onto the ground and push it. They crawled over the steep slope, David pulling, Mike pushing, just like before. It took hours, my dad tells me. "We looked like the Egyptians building the pyramids, moving that heavy boat around." The floodwall conquered, the boys loaded the boat back onto the wagon and rolled down the quiet alley behind their house into their backyard.

Their prize hidden behind the beagle pen, Mike and David walked to the local hardware store for a tube of liquid solder. Over the next few days, the boys scrubbed the boat clean and squeezed the bonding agent into the cracks in the flat metal bottom. Every day, they dumped water into the boat, and when it leaked out onto the grass, they dried the boat off and patched it again. My dad says Elwood must have noticed what they were up to, but he didn't try to stop them. Maybe he understood the boys' yearning for a dangerous water adventure.

Finally, the patches held, and the boys scrounged up some paddles. The next morning they lifted the boat onto their now bent-up wagon and headed back over the floodwall to the river. They didn't bother with bologna or fishing poles. It was all about the boat. When they got to the bank, they waited for a barge to pass by, and then they slid the boat down through the mud into the river and climbed in, pushing off against the rocky riverbed with their paddles. Mike took the steering position in the back and David paddled from the front, the same positions they take in the summers now when they canoe together between the high rock walls of the Potomac River trench, peering up at bald eagles and clouds.

As the brothers plunged their paddles again and again, propelling themselves across the murky river, they whispered about future fishing trips and excursions in their boat. Then cool river water started soaking their cotton shorts. Mike grabbed David's paddle and pushed for the closest bank—the Ohio side—and yelled for David to bail. David did bail—he can't remember what with—and somehow they made it to the bank. They dragged the leaky boat up onto the riverbank and tramped around for a few minutes on their new territory: a backyard in Ohio.

Then they realized they had to get home. At first, the boys imagined themselves walking back, rambling along the riverbank, crossing a bridge on foot, but then they remembered the nearest bridge was fifteen miles away. It'd take till nightfall, even on a long July day, to get back to their house. They didn't want to knock on the front door of one of the riverfront houses—their fists leaving damp spots under the seasonal wreath—and ask to use the phone. They'd have to bother their dad at work and tell him what they'd gotten themselves into; their mom didn't have a car. So, they crossed the river again, Mike paddling, David bailing. When they got back to West Virginia, they stepped out onto dry land and let the boat sink back into the river.

Three

When I was in my early teens, my dad, Jennifer, Rebecca, and I decided to canoe all the way across Beech Fork Lake in Lavalette, West Virginia, an undertaking we knew would take a day of paddling in the blistering August heat. Maybe my dad was thinking fondly of that time he and Mike had boated all the way across the Ohio River, imagining their old rowboat still rusting away on the riverbed, but my sisters and I hadn't yet heard that story. We just wanted to do it. We had often put on our heavy nylon life jackets and canoed for a couple of miles along the lake's shady perimeter, enjoying the wildlife we could view best from a silent resting place out on the water. From our canoe, we'd watched a red-and-black water snake thread across the brown rippling surface and a mother turkey and her little flock peck in the tall grass along the water's edge. But we wanted to go further, see more. We wanted to get in the canoe and actually go somewhere: the Beech Fork campground on the other side of the lake.

We'd driven to the campground before, but not often. For our weekend hikes and fishing trips, we stuck to a section of the state park close to our home, climbing the steep trails and casting from a boat dock far across the lake from the bustling campground's RVs and bathhouses. But every summer, Grandpa's side of the family holds the Childers family reunion at the campground, and we wend our way down winding, washed out, trailer-lined roads to eat fried chicken and casseroles under a picnic shelter. When we get to those reunions, I sit on a bench in the heat with a can of Coke, too nauseated from the car ride to listen to my elderly relatives tell stories, but I understand why we hold the reunion where we do. Several decades before the state government bought the land for the park and created a lake for flood control, a piece of that land was Grandpa's family farm.

A few Childers reunions ago, after we threw away our plastic plates and cutlery, my siblings, my dad, and I piled into Grandpa's sedan and rode past the RVs to the part of the lake where the farm used to be. "If you look real hard over there," Grandpa said, pointing along the lakeshore to a patch of briars and trees, "you can still see one of the trees from our old apple orchard." He stared at an overgrown tree I couldn't quite make out, seeing tidy rows of fruit trees and a few half-ripe apples on the mown grass, knocked from their branches by a thunderstorm. Then we climbed back into the car, and Grandpa drove us down a gravel road to the weedy cemetery where our ancestors lie.

Before the state government flooded river water over the farms, filling the valleys between the oak- and maple-covered hills, workers exhumed the bodies buried here and there under little clumps of family headstones. They reburied the old coffins in a local cemetery beyond the water's reach, gathering the land's deceased inhabitants in an underground reunion of their own. Now, it's difficult to tell which of the mossy slabs of marble have rested there since the 1800s and which migrated to the plot in the 1970s. My siblings and I wandered through the graveyard, trying to keep our flip-flops from disappearing into the mud as Grandpa gave us the tour. He paused in front of his aunts' and uncles' graves, stooping with a twig to knock soil and fallen leaves from their markers.

The morning of the trip, a month after that year's reunion, my dad, my sisters, and I rose early to dig the life jackets, canvas flotation pillows, my dad's fishing pole, and the canoe paddles from the storage building and pack a red Igloo cooler with the heat-survival menu I'd chosen: root beer, bologna sandwiches, bottled water, and Snickers bars. Then the four of us carried the canoe down our backyard hill to the driveway, where we hoisted the aluminum boat on top of our green minivan and strapped it to the luggage rack. We drove to the marina, past goats, new vinyl-sided subdivisions, and trailer parks, and we carried the canoe down the concrete boat ramp into the water. We set off, pushing against the ramp with our paddles to gain momentum. My dad steered from the metal seat in the back of the boat, I paddled away up front, and Jennifer and Rebecca settled against the cooler on the flotation pillows we used as the third and fourth seats. My sisters scanned the hills for rare songbirds and deer and chatted quietly about boys.

Our first moments on the lake were glorious: we paddled in the morning sun, paused in quiet coves to drink root beer, and fished for bluegill and sunfish. We untangled the hooks from pearly fish lips and let our catch flash back underwater to sulk between rocks on the lakebed. The lake meanders between the hills, so we couldn't see our destination as we floated across the water, and we reveled at first in the idea that we were questing without a map, uncertain of exactly how we'd find the campground. Each bend in the lake revealed new sights: great blue herons in pterodactyl-like flight and red and pink lilies, lonely survivors of flooded-out gardens. Less possessive about the steering than his brother Mike, my dad let us take turns paddling from the rear seat, aiming the canoe toward the setting of so many of Grandpa's stories.

But as the day crept by, my sisters and I became aware of the intensifying heat, how much root beer we'd drunk, and how tight our youth-sized life jackets had grown since we'd bought them several years before. Still, we were out on the lake with our dad in the summer, and we had a goal to reach. We wanted to drift over the ground where Grandpa used to milk his father's cows, and we wanted to use the camping area's walled-in flush toilets instead of burying ourselves in a thick patch of weeds beside the lake, hoping to avoid the eyes of unseen anglers. We paddled on.

By the third hour, we'd emptied the cooler of all liquids but a single bottle of water, our muscles ached, and the sun glared from its one p.m. perch. My sisters and I started trailing our fingers and long brown hair in the lake and asking how far we were from the toilets and pop machines. Gunshots interrupted our whining, louder and closer than the usual distant rumble of illegal hunters in the park. "At least now we know where we are," my dad said, lowering his head and paddling faster from the back. "We must be getting close to that firing range on the other side of the park."

"Aah!" Jennifer wailed, pointing to a row of bright orange signs on the shore, their metal poles tangled in ivy. "We're going to get shot! Turn around, Daddy. Turn around!" The signs, riddled with rifle shot, warned hikers, boaters, and fishermen that they'd crossed into dangerous proximity of the firing range.

"No, we've got to be almost to the campground. All you girls have to pee, right?"

"Yes," we muttered, watching the woods for crazed men with rifles.

"Well, we're going to make it to those bathrooms. Paddle harder, Sarah Beth!"

My sisters covered their heads with their sunburned hands, and my dad and I dug our paddles deep into the lake water and barreled past the signs. After a few minutes, the gunshots faded under the sounds of birdcalls, cicadas, and motorboat engines.

We were safe, but the campground was nowhere in sight. Every muscle-burning bend brought another stretch of brown water and trees. Finally, we floated under a place that looked familiar: a bridge on a road that led to the campground. My dad parked the canoe between the concrete pilings and scaled the hill, using his paddle as a walking stick. As he stood on the asphalt, looking for landmarks up and down the road, my sisters and I giggled at the lost explorer with his life jacket, yellow-tipped paddle, and Marshall University ball cap. After a minute, he slid back down the hill, looking discouraged.

"Well, I was hoping I'd spot some place with a pay phone so we could call your mother and ask her to come rescue us, but there's nothing, and I haven't got a clue where we are," he said. "You girls better pee under that bridge, and we'll turn around and head back."

"No," I insisted, cringing at the thought of the sharp rocks and the wad of now-damp toilet paper I'd brought along in my pocket. "Let's go just a little further."

I took over the steering and we paddled on, and after five minutes, a circle of RVs and a few rickety brown buildings glowed on the shore. We jumped out onto the bank and dragged the canoe up onto the grass, then we threw our life jackets into the boat and ran for those brown buildings, elated. I could see a pop machine by the restroom door. A few minutes later, refreshed, cold cans of Pepsi in hand, my sisters and I walked more casually back to the canoe, feeling superior to the camper kids who were playing Frisbee with their golden retrievers. We'd arrived by boat, after all, and they'd just come in their parents' trucks and RVs.

Our dad waited by the canoe, already wearing his life jacket, looking grim. "I didn't see a pay phone, did you?"

"Nope," we said. I ran back to the bathroom and looked around, just in case we'd missed it, but no phone.

"Let's get back in the canoe," my dad said, cracking open the can of Pepsi I'd brought him. We settled back onto the metal seats and canvas cushions and paddled for the firing range.

The Tricia Has Crashed

WHEN I DROVE MY GRANDPARENTS from Huntington, West Virginia, to Philadelphia to watch their youngest son die, I played and replayed a forty-year-old, home-recorded cassette. Outside the car, darkness obscured black-and-white cows, much-needed road signs, and gas stations that had closed for the night.

On the tape, the sun is rising. Three healthy boys—ages nine, fourteen, and nineteen—stand in a dewy field, halfway between a rickety baseball stadium and a litter-strewn stream.

The boys are launching model rockets. They've built the rockets themselves, scavenging in their parents' cabinets for materials. A wrapping paper tube for the body, a circular scrap of trash bag for the parachute. Mike, the oldest, narrates the launch. "This is the flight of the C_1," he says, his voice serious as if he's recording a NASA experiment. "Recovery crews are taking their positions." He means David, my dad.

Mark, the youngest, mans a small plywood box, ready to launch the rocket with the push of a button. The box connects to the launchpad with a fifteen-foot wire, so Mark's brothers have draped a ratty carpet over his head, protecting him from explosions and flyaway balsawood nose cones. Mark and Mike exchange signals, and a flashlight bulb on the box illuminates. "We have continuity," Mike declares. A pause.

A *whoosh!* The rocket zips off the launchpad and sails above the treetops, above the rotten canvas roof of the baseball stadium. "We have liftoff." Mike stops the recording and David hunts down the rocket, sprinting as the parachute floats north on the breeze. The rocket, now a snarl of bag, kite string, cardboard, and balsa, lands on the grass at the edge of the clearing. A few yards to the left, and the rocket would have dangled from the high limb of an oak; Mike would have sent David up to fetch it.

David dashes back with the rocket to his older brother, who takes it and presses *Record*.

"Beautiful flight," Mike crows, inspecting the tube under the half-risen sun. "The condition of the rocket is perfect."

"Beautiful flight," MaMa warbled in the car. "What about that." She switched on the dome light and rummaged through her pocketbook for another Tic Tac. "Didn't you say Mark was on this tape?"

"Yes, MaMa, in just a minute." I turned up the volume. "Daddy is talking right now."

David narrates his launch with shy enthusiasm; he doesn't sound as NASA-ready as his older brother. Just before the *whoosh*, David hollers, "Here it goes!" Mike would have said, "We have liftoff."

The rocket whooshes up, but it plummets back down. The engine has failed to blow off the nose cone, so the parachute waits, neatly folded, inside the cardboard tube. David yells, "It's falling! It's falling. It's falling." He pauses after each *falling*, face upturned, as if he's trying to catch the rocket with his voice. Then he yelps, "Mark!"

Mark dodges the missile and takes a turn at the tape recorder, narrating the flight of two rockets named after Mike's girlfriend, Patricia. "This is the flight of the *Big Patti*," Mark begins, and he counts down loudly. His West Virginia accent, stronger than I ever heard it, gives every number two syllables. "Fah-ive, fow-ur, tha-ree, ta-oo, woh-un. Zee-row." The rocket zips off, and Mark loses interest in the tape, forgetting to tell posterity if the flight was beautiful or not. A few minutes later, he begins afresh with a new rocket. "This is the flight of the *Tricia*." He counts down, softly this time, and after a few moments he shrieks with giggles. "The *Tricia* has crashed!" he announces. He sounds jubilant, like he had been waiting all morning for that crash.

When the tape came to the part when Mark begins to speak, my grandparents often forgot to listen. They talked about what the doctor had said the morning before, when he'd called about their faraway son's cirrhosis of the liver. They talked about the way Mark had sounded on the phone. "Just like a little baby," MaMa said. "Some nurse brought him his dinner, and he asked me, 'Can I eat now?'" When she raised her voice an octave and slowed her speech—*Can . . . I . . . eat . . . now?*—she drowned out the real child-voice on the tape.

I rewound a few inches of tape and pushed play again. "Listen, Mark's about to talk." Listen, I begged. Listen to your well and happy son. Out in a field in the morning with his brothers.

✦ ✦ ✦

THE evenings before the boys launched rockets, Mike picked up David and Mark and drove them to his apartment across town. The brothers sat on Mike's brown shag carpet and worked until two in the morning.

Mike had trained his younger brothers to help with just about everything. David and Mark held a wrapping paper tube against the inside front of Mike's sock drawer, using the right angle to trace notches for attaching the fins. They cut rings from a sheet of balsawood and slid them inside the tube, then they friction-fitted the engine inside the rings. For a perfect friction fit, too snug for the engine to fly out with the parachute, they rolled the little cylinder in notebook paper and layers of masking tape.

Mike had also taught David and Mark to fashion the nose cone. They cut balsawood into long, thin isosceles triangles that met at a point and fanned out in a circle. Originally, Mike had tried a faster method of nose cone production, spinning a block of balsa on a drill and holding it up to a piece of sandpaper. They'd attached the lumpy result to a rocket christened *The Thumb,* and Mike had headed back to the drawing board.

While his brothers finished the rocket bodies, Mike adjusted the insides of the plywood box, a nine-volt-battery-powered launching system he'd designed himself. My dad said he never understood that box; "it seemed like it was full of magic." When the box worked correctly, Mike pulled a chain on the box and sent a charge around a circuit. The flashlight bulb on top of the box lit up, and the boys were ready for the morning launch. Mike loaded his sleepy brothers into his car and drove them back across town.

Three hours later, David woke up to knuckles on glass. By climbing the front porch railing, Mike could just reach the bottom of his brother's bedroom window. David sprang up and tiptoed past his parents' bedroom door to the bathroom, where he squeezed his eyes shut and splashed water on his face, frigid as the faucet would allow. Then David slipped into Mark's room and uncovered his little brother. He picked up Mark and stood him on his feet, and then he marshaled him into the bathroom and turned on the cold water.

Cold water had been the brothers' secret wake-up ritual since they were tiny boys, setting an alarm clock for dawn so they could walk down to the Ohio River and go fishing. The three boys had shared a room, sleeping in beds their father had crafted from old doors. When little David crawled off his door, he staggered and moaned. "Just splash some cold water on your face," Mike told him. "You'll wake right up." David believed this fervidly, because Mike had said it. But he never felt really awake until he plopped down on a damp log and plunged his soles into the river.

Launching rockets, David felt awake when the first rocket whooshed and his older brother said, "We have liftoff."

+ + +

AS the rocket tape played, I drove past Dutch Wonderland, an Amish-themed amusement park, and miles of pitch-black barns and cornfields. Finally, I found a Turkey Hill gas station that was open all night. Grandpa pumped the gas, and I headed inside to buy ice cream bars that met MaMa's specifications. "Chocolate, honey, but you better get me a soft one or it'll tear out my partial."

Back on the road, wiping ice cream from our fingers, we all felt too cheerful to restart the tape, to hear the little boy voice that was so nearly a ghost. I asked my grandparents to tell stories.

MaMa told me about the Great Depression, when her father lost his job at the glass factory. For years, he'd stood next to a furnace and blown through a tube, inflating molten glass like a balloon. Then he'd clamped the luminous orange bubble into a mold and blown again. When the glass cooled, he'd opened the mold and lifted out a vase or a lamp.

The glass factory had paid well, allowing Emma's—my grandmother's—father to build a house with a freestanding staircase and enough room to accommodate his four boys and six girls. The front parlor had had fine carpets and a piano. When Emma's father lost his job, he sold the house before the bank could think about taking it, and he bought a smaller place across town. In the new house, Emma slept in the attic, sharing a bed with all five of her sisters. In the summers, the girls spent their nights squirming away from each other's sweaty bodies, escaping one sister's leg by rolling against the sticky nightgown on another sister's back. When a sister got up to pee, the others waited a minute for the empty place to cool. Then they all dove for that sweaty patch of sheets. The creaking bedsprings kept time with the girls' shifting weight. The winning sister closed her eyes with a smug smile, enjoying her moment of relief.

Grandpa yarned about his own attic bedroom, in the farmhouse where his family lived when he was little. Elwood slept alone in a tiny bed, next to a hole in the roof that let in breezes, moonlight, and whiffs of cow manure. One of his brothers slept in a crib downstairs; his youngest brother hadn't yet been born. When a full moon lit up the attic, Elwood carefully unfolded his treasure: the funny paper he kept under his mattress so his little brother wouldn't crumple it. He had no idea newspapers printed new comics every day; he believed these strips contained the only tales of Li'l Abner, Snuffy Smith, and Little Orphan Annie. He read those stories and chuckled to himself, thinking how lucky he was to have the comics.

And then Grandpa told another story. When Mark was in his late teens, Elwood and Emma took him on a trip to visit Mike, who had married Patricia and found work as a physics teacher in Virginia. David didn't go on that trip; maybe he was too busy with college or with courting my mother. On the long car ride home, Mark stretched his body across the backseat—three seats all to himself—and went to sleep.

Hours later, Mark woke up to his mother's screams. Night had fallen, and the headlights illuminated a concrete column. Elwood was asleep at the wheel on the highway, and instead of driving under a bridge, Elwood was driving *into* it. Mark lay back down on the seat, covered his shaggy blond head with his arms, and curled his legs to his chest. Emma smacked Elwood and woke him up; he slammed the brakes and cut the wheel, just in time.

After Elwood straightened the tires and got back up to speed—just another car on the highway at night—Mark gasped, "Is it over?" His voice sounded small, like a child's. Emma turned and looked at her son; he still had his arms over his head. Maybe he was thinking he was captain of his high school cross-country team, but he still didn't have a girlfriend. He planned to go to West Virginia University and study agriculture. He might inherit a yellow Datsun from his brother.

"Yes," Emma said. She reached over the seat and touched his hair. "It's over. We're going to a motel."

✦ ✦ ✦

IT was late when we reached the Philadelphia suburbs, so the three of us crammed into a motel bed and slept. We *could* sleep because we hadn't seen Mark yet. Our stomachs hadn't begun their grinding, ulcerous calculations of how much time with him we'd lose if we lay down for a short rest, if we went down to the cafeteria for a sandwich.

We hadn't seen Mark in three years. In the past, Mark had often traveled to Huntington in the summers, and he'd always come home for Christmas. Gathered in their parents' living room, the brothers had unwrapped gifts for the cheap, practical outdoorsman: wool shirts and socks, flashlights from a clearance rack, fishing hats that could float.

The last Christmas Mark came home, the brothers had unearthed a yellowed list of study tips. A few years before the boys launched their rockets, the list had hung on Mark's bedroom wall. Little Mark had liked to catch one of his teenage brothers on the toilet and read him the tips through the bathroom door. "Have a regular time and place. Keep your glasses spotlessly clean. Apply the material to your daily life." Middle-aged Mike and David gasped with laughter as Mark read the list aloud.

But Mark had been too ill for three Christmases to drive those nine hours home. Too ill in body and mind with something he'd hidden, for more than a decade, perhaps, until Mark's doctor told Elwood and Emma about their son's corroded liver. For three years, Mark hadn't let anyone visit him. "If you drive up here," he'd told us, "I'm bolting my door." He'd suffered in private, leaving nothing for his family to do but sit with him while he died.

When we entered Mark's hospital room, we stared for a minute, making sure we'd found the correct dying man. He'd been overweight the last time I saw him, and now he was skinny as the pictures of his cross-country days, though fluid swelled his belly like a pregnancy. His arms, once strong enough to hoist a canoe onto his car, seemed as tiny and delicate as a toddler's. His once trim blond beard hung in a thick mat over his chest, like the beards of the homeless men who met in the Huntington library for a chat. But on close inspection, that was Mark's broad nose, and Mike had mailed him that hat in the corner.

"Mark? We're here," MaMa said at last. She placed her hand on the sheets beside her son's feet. "You sang 'Happy Mother's Day' to me so beautifully, just two weeks ago. It's on our answering machine. You sang it like 'Happy Birthday.' So loud and clear!"

Mark pressed his needle-bruised fists into the bed and grimaced. He had his thick bifocals on, but his eyes looked unfocused. I wasn't sure he could see us.

"It's us, Mark. It's Sarah Beth, and Mom and Dad. Mike and David are coming tomorrow." I didn't know if they'd be coming tomorrow, or if they'd be able to leave their jobs at all. But I had to tell Mark they'd be there. With my dad's straight hair and too-wide smile, I felt like a paltry stand-in for Mark's brother. I knew Mark loved my siblings and me. He'd loved us especially when we were children, and he could pile gifts for us under his parents' Christmas tree until he'd hid a third of the boughs.

But I knew I wasn't enough. Mark needed his brothers, the other two voices on the tape. Mark could man the plywood box, but he needed David to hunt the rocket down, and Mike to design the rocket in the first place. "We're here," I repeated. "Mike and David are coming."

After a few long moments, Mark dug his fists into the sheets again, determined this time to sit up. "Coffee," he said, his voice small. "I'd like some coffee."

Glad to feel useful, I jogged down the hall to the nurse's station and found Mark's nurse, a young, red-haired woman with a constant, too-sympathetic smile.

"He's not supposed to have any," she said. She lowered her voice and freshened her smile. "It'll upset his stomach. And coffee won't wake him up. That poison from his liver is making him sleepy, and he's just going to get sleepier until, you know."

I did know, but I insisted, and the nurse filled a Styrofoam cup. My uncle had ordered us not to visit him; that coffee meant he wanted to see us.

+ + +

THREE days later, I called my dad from the hospital hallway. *Daddy, you've got to get up here.* I meant it for myself as much as Mark. From the moment we'd entered the hospital, I'd barely slept or eaten, and I'd repeated everything for my half-deaf grandparents. Questions they asked each other, updates from the nurses, anything Mark muttered, awake or asleep.

"What did she say, honey?"

"What did that man tell us, Sarah Beth?"

They're taking Mark's blood pressure, MaMa. The Hospice people will be here this afternoon. Grandpa said he was going to the bathroom.

It was hardest when I had to tell them something Mark had said, and the words were too heartbreaking to repeat. A doctor came by and spoke to Mark's roommate, an elderly Italian man, about his upcoming gallbladder surgery. Mark heard it all through the thin striped curtain, and he thought the news was meant for him.

"A procedure?" Mark asked through the curtain. His voice suddenly sounded as strong as it had three years before, when he'd read his list of study tips beside the Christmas tree. "You didn't tell me about a procedure! When is it?" The doctor ignored him. When the doctor left, Mark pushed the call button and demanded an update. "When's my surgery? Is it tonight? Why won't you nurses answer me?"

"I'll be there in a minute," Mark's nurse chirped finally, a sigh in her chirp.

As Mark waited, he folded his hands over his chest and smiled to himself. "I thought I was finished, and now I'm going to have a procedure."

MaMa caught the last word. "What's he talking about, honey? What procedure?" I didn't know how to explain.

I wanted my dad and uncle there to hear it all with me. I was tired of repeating everything to Mark's parents in his room, to his brothers over the phone. I needed to escape the terrible responsibility of deciding what everyone knew.

+ + +

EVERY time Mark pressed the button to launch a rocket, the brothers hoped for a crash. They'd mastered the art of rocket making too quickly: Mike's magic box, the balsawood nose cone, the fireproof wadding paper that kept the parachute from burning up. They felt proud when the rockets shot straight into the air, the nose cones popped off right on time, and the rockets descended gracefully on their parachutes. But those beautiful flights got boring after a while. The boys got tired of happy endings, just like I did as a child reader, when I wished all those perpetually lucky characters would break their legs, never recover their lost parakeets, or starve at the bottoms of wells.

Estes engines nearly always worked, so the brothers bought cheaper ones on purpose. The cheap engines worked fine for two launches out of three, but on that third launch, anything might happen. Some rockets plummeted like the *Tricia:* the engine launched the rocket, but failed to send out that second charge that blew off the nose cone and opened the parachute. Other rockets sailed up a few feet and exploded, raining ash onto Mark's carpet-draped head. And a few rockets blew up on the launchpad.

On the rocket tape, after the *Tricia* slams into the ground, Mike narrates another launch. He loads a fresh engine into the C1, a rocket that had flown beautifully earlier that morning. Mike exchanges signals with Mark and declares, "We have continuity." He counts down from ten to zero. But instead of a *whoosh*, the tape captured a soft *boom*. After a couple of stunned seconds, Mike starts to laugh.

"The rocket blew *up!* In a big puff of *smoke!*" Mike's voice swings upward at the end of each line as he chuckles out the words. When C1 had flown beautifully, he'd reported the news like a calm professional. But now, staring at the charred remains of that cardboard tube and parachute the boys had worked on all night, Mike sounds as giddy as Mark or David. "The body of the rocket is *very* badly damaged. And that's the last flight of the C1."

+ + +

TWO days after my frantic phone call, Mike and David arrived at the hospital. Mike had told David on the drive there that he couldn't do any "bedside sitting." He planned to deal with the problems he might be able to fix. He'd clear the dying man's junk out of Mark's apartment before a lawyer or landlord saw it. Scrub the blood from Mark's bathroom floor. Search for unpaid bills. Let David watch from a vinyl chair as his brother's body shut down. Let David languish like Mary at Jesus's feet. Mike was Martha, and he was ready to get to work.

But when the brothers arrived, Mike walked into the hospital room. I offered my chair to my uncle, but he wouldn't take it; he stood in the shaft of sunlight between the window and the bed. Mark didn't stir when his brothers came in. Mike took a step back toward the door, whispering that maybe he'd see Mark later, when he was awake.

"No," I whispered. "He's always sleepy because of his liver. I'm sure he'll want to see you." Then, more loudly, I said, "Mark! Mike and David are here!" They were both there, though my dad hadn't entered the room. He'd seen his brother's bruised skin and swollen belly and stopped in the doorway, covering his grimace with a shaking hand. I'd seen that look on my dad's face once before, after little Joshua got hit by the bicycle, and I'd carried my brother into the house with his tibia poking through his leg.

Mark groaned and shifted, then said, "Hi, Mike, David." His voice was weak, but I could hear the lilting tone he used when he greeted his brothers at Christmas.

"You look like an old hippie dude," Mike said, looking at his brother's long hair and beard. Then he propped himself against the wall and told a story. "On the way here, David and I stopped for some sandwiches at a grocery store, and now my stomach's feeling funny. That was a lot of meat and cheese." He opened his hand wide and looked into it, as if the sandwich still rested there.

"Meat and cheese. Hum," Mike continued, staring thoughtfully at the imaginary sandwich. "That reminds me of that time, more than thirty years ago now, that me and you and David were out fishing. We were just about starved, and we stopped and got those big sandwiches. Now *that* was a lot of meat and cheese." Mike paused, allowing the memory to float out into the air, the scene to take solid form inside the hospital room. Suddenly, the brothers were on a fishing trip. Mike was twenty-five; David, twenty; Mark, fifteen.

"Yep, I remember that!" Mark said, chuckling lightly. "That was a good sandwich."

"Oh, right!" David said. He left the doorway and stood beside the bed. "We were out on that gravel road in the mountains, feeling like we were about to pass out, and then we found that gas station in the middle of nowhere. We went in thinking we could get a bag of chips, and then that old man said he could make us all a sandwich. He took out slices of bread and just *loaded* on the bologna. Biggest sandwich I ever had!"

"Yep!' said Mark, nodding. In Mark's face, I could see a concrete floor, splotchy with mud from fishermen's boots. An old man making sandwiches at a deli counter, between a refrigerator full of nightcrawlers and a shelf of engine oil. "He had those big, thick pieces of cheese."

Then Mike headed out to clean Mark's apartment. David sat by the bed for thirty-six hours, until Mark could no longer speak.

+ + +

I launched rockets with my dad and sisters at Beech Fork State Park, in a field bordered by a creek, a grass-covered dam, and a deep valley filled with maples. I was twelve, Jennifer nine, Rebecca six. On the way out the door, I hugged Joshua, then three, who stayed home to play with his Disney Dwarves. Sneezy's nose reddened and Grumpy's eyebrows grew dark and menacing when Joshua soaked the dolls in a pail of water. I squealed, "We're going to launch rockets!" and covered his honey-sticky face with kisses.

At the park, my dad took out his pocketknife and slit open a model rocket kit, one of my Christmas gifts from Mark. While my sisters wandered, wriggling with impatience, my dad and I sat on the grass, surrounded by the kit's contents: a prepainted rocket body, a plastic nose cone, a red-and-white parachute a tiny plastic man might use to skydive. My dad tossed aside the sheet of directions and started fitting the pieces together.

"We'll have this thing together in no time," he said. Compared with my dad's childhood launch preparations, we did put the rocket together quickly, but our building process took long enough to make me feel intelligent and important. I crammed protective wadding into the rocket body and applied white, donut-shaped reinforcements to the holes in the parachute. My dad threaded the parachute with kite string and selected an Estes engine from our stash. My dad always bought those dull, reliable Estes engines; maybe it didn't feel right to blow up his daughters' toys.

Finally, my dad set up the launchpad and popped the batteries into the black plastic launcher. I yelled for my sisters, loudly enough for other park-goers to hear. "Come *on!* We're ready to launch a rocket!" Rebecca trotted back first, her hands full of the dandelions, violets, and clover blossoms she'd picked for me to string into a necklace. Then Jennifer appeared, her waist-length hair dripping algae; she'd been combing puddles for tadpoles she could take home in a jar.

My dad closed his fist over the top of the tall, narrow launch rod and squatted down beside the launchpad. "My brother Mike taught me this. If you're ever standing close to the launchpad and you need to bend down, you have to cover up the rod. Otherwise, you might poke your eye out." Then he slid the rocket down the rod and handed the controller to me. "Jennifer, Rebecca! Stand back!" he said.

Ten, nine. We all counted down together. I pushed the button, and the rocket whooshed higher than the playground's enormous yellow slide, the paved crest of the dam, the flirting finches. I thought the nose cone brushed a cloud. My sisters and I jumped and whooped, our necks craned until they hurt. We imagined ourselves inside the rocket, looking down at the park from the sky.

Thirty years earlier and twelve miles away, Mike, David, and Mark caught dragonflies on the grassy floodwall in the summer and slid home on a piece of cardboard. In the winter, they took their Flexible Flyer from the storage shed and trudged up the floodwall, mussing the snow with boot prints and the slim tracks of the sled's steel runners. Usually, the boys rode down feet first, one or two at a time. Sometimes Mike sat at the back of the sled, steering with his tennis shoes, and Mark squeezed in between his legs. But one day, the boys decided they should all pile onto the sled: three brothers at once, headfirst.

Before the boys sailed down the hill, they had to decide where they wanted to go. They could aim the sled toward the oaks, briers, and near-freezing water on the river side of the wall, or toward the telephone poles, parked cars, and cinder-block foundations on the neighborhood side. The boys aimed their sled toward the river and climbed on. Mike stretched out over the wooden slats; he was the biggest, and he wanted to steer. David stretched out over his older brother, and Mark lay on top, clinging through his mittens to David's coat.

As Mike tested the steering, nudging the wooden cross-bar left and right, his younger brothers huddled through their parkas and two layers of pants, soaking in each other's warmth. Then Mike kicked with his boots and yelled at David to push off with his gloves, and the sled teetered at the top. A few more pushes and a mighty kick, and the boys whizzed down the floodwall. David's and Mark's eyeglasses blurred with snowflakes and breath. As the sled flew, the boys calculated how soon they'd need to roll off into the snow, so they wouldn't slam into a tree or plop into the river. They didn't have to roll off. Three-quarters of the way down, the sled skidded sideways, dumping the boys and sliding down without them. The two older boys untangled their limbs and stood up, cold but okay.

But Mark was missing. Looking around, Mike and David saw bare branches weighed down with white, the dark brown river between the trees. They saw their own awkward snow angels, evidence of their spill from the sled. And they saw the snowdrifts at the bottom of the floodwall, deep enough for a small boy to slide inside and disappear. The boys ran down the hill and froze their wet-gloved fingers, digging for their little brother in the snow.

+ + +

THE day Mark died, we sat with him at the Hospice House, in a room with soft chairs, big windows to let in sunshine, and no doctors discussing surgeries behind a curtain. Mike and David had gone back to work, so it was just my grandparents and me. We'd stopped pretending to talk to Mark; his nose and cheeks looked flattened, and his mouth hung open in a perpetual raspy breath.

MaMa told me she had "a hankering for a softie," meaning a chocolate Frosty from Wendy's. My grandparents had barely eaten since the first morning they saw their son, so I circled nearby blocks until I found a Wendy's. I made it back to Hospice and held up the cold paper cup, triumphant. "I got you a softie!" But Mark was dead.

We'd planned to spend the night in the Hospice House, on the hideaway bed and recliners in Mark's room. When Mark died, the nurses folded up the bed and stashed our blankets and pillows in the closet. "We need to get ready for our next patient. You'll have to stay somewhere else." Grandpa didn't want to stay somewhere else. His youngest son had just died, and finding a motel was more than he could bear. We got in the car and headed for West Virginia.

I was driving. I knew I couldn't make it all the way to Huntington, but I figured I could make it to my apartment in Morgantown, West Virginia, five hours from the Philadelphia suburbs and four hours from home. I bought a large iced tea at every service plaza on the turnpike and asked my grandparents about the Great Depression, the letters they wrote during the war, anything that might keep me awake.

Two hours from Morgantown, I ran out of iced tea and stopped at a service plaza for more. The plaza's Starbucks and convenience store had closed for the night, and we hadn't seen a fast food joint in miles. I bawled and told Grandpa I couldn't drive anymore.

"I'll do it!" he said. "Just two hours, and we've got to get home. We've got a funeral to plan." He sounded chipper to me, and he looked a lot more awake than my bleary reflection in the rearview mirror. I surrendered the driver's seat and the keys.

I should have realized this was a bad idea. Grandpa's son had just died, and he hadn't eaten or slept in a week. After a few miles, he had to pass through a tollbooth, and he drove into a lane meant for cars heading the opposite direction. I gripped the seat as he backed up, thanking God there were no cars on the road.

I tried to keep Grandpa talking. Tell me about the time you saw MaMa at the movie theater, when you were nine. Tell me about that duck you kept on the ship in the navy. But halfway through a story, I must have drifted off. When I woke up, Grandpa was asleep, and the car was zigzagging in and out of the passing lane. I felt like I'd slipped into Grandpa's story, the one with Grandpa asleep at the wheel and teenage Mark in the backseat, except Mark was dead, and MaMa was too exhausted to scream. Grandpa woke up a few seconds too late; the car hit the median, rolled twice, and landed upside down. My head pressed against the ceiling, haloed by loose change and one of my shoes.

I asked my grandparents if they were okay—miraculously, they were, nothing broken—and then the shock set in. I crawled out of the car and stepped onto the interstate in my socks. I bolted across the median, ran laps around the lanes. The pavement felt cool and hard through the knitted cotton. "It's my fault!" I screamed.

I couldn't remember we were alive. Mark had died, then it seemed we'd had this wreck and died, too. An empty couch and an empty wingback on Christmas morning. A truck driver parked his semi, ran onto the road, and caught me. "Stop runnin,' darlin,'" he said, pinning my arms to my sides. "You're gonna get yourself killed." I broke free and raced across the road again, blackening my socks with each step. *It's my fault. It's my fault.*

Maybe if I ran fast enough, I could hurry back and stop the wreck. I'd return to that service plaza and insist we go to a motel, or take a nap in the parking lot and keep driving the car myself.

My dad and his brothers had hoped for explosions at the ends of model rocket launches. I'd wished for dead children at the ends of books. But in our real lives, we wanted the sleeping driver to wake up, or just stay awake in the first place. We dug for our brothers in the snow.

During those moments when I suspected I was dead, I thought about my siblings, imagining away myself. Only two little girls at the rocket launches. Just two young women and a teenage boy on a picnic bench on a Sunday afternoon. Jennifer, Rebecca, and Joshua would learn how it feels to lose a sibling. I would never have to know.

Kite String

I KNEW MY UNCLE MARK HAD BEEN HAPPY sometimes when I saw the kites in the trunk of his car. After Mark died, his ten-year-old Honda Civic rode south to West Virginia on the back of a truck. The interior was cleaner than I'd expected from his illness and fast food habits—a ball cap in the backseat, loose change in the cup holders—so my curiosity shifted to the trunk. As my dad fiddled with the lock, I huddled with my grandparents in their driveway, my stomach tightening with fearful excitement.

A couple of months earlier, I'd had that same feeling in my stomach when I creaked open the door to Mark's apartment in the Philadelphia suburbs. Mark was sleeping in his hospital room a few miles away, unaware that his parents and I had taken his keys from the pocket of his sweatpants. We were hoping, vainly, to find his apartment clean enough that we could let him die at home.

When I was furnishing my first apartment, Mark had told me, half embarrassed, half boasting, that he'd never needed any furniture but a bed, a chair, and a stand for the TV. The chair in question was a stained orange velveteen rocker, surrounded by empty glass bottles and plastic cups, evidence of the addiction that had devoured his liver, swelled his legs and stomach, and finally killed him. An addiction he'd hidden from us until that moment. "That chair looks as good as it did the day I gave it to him!" MaMa said when she saw it. Her bifocals must have been failing her, but I let it pass. After a few minutes in Mark's apartment, I had to run back out to the parking lot, shaking with grief.

When my dad opened Mark's trunk, two months after he died, I cringed, expecting to find a forgotten bottle of Jim Beam, cooked in the July heat, or a pile of liquor store receipts. But inside the trunk were only relics of the Mark we'd known: fishing tackle, country music CDs, scruffy shoes and vinyl pants for wading in streams. My dad had become a crier when he'd seen his dying brother in the hospital. After he opened Mark's trunk, he wept again from joy and relief. He fingered a fuchsia-and-yellow kite that lay on top of the pile. He said, "I guess Mark kept all the sad stuff in his apartment and all the happy stuff in here."

✢ ✢ ✢

WHEN David and his brothers were children, they flew kites on the ridge of the grassy floodwall. Mike took charge, David followed instructions, and Mark tagged along. Mike was expert at putting kites together from kits, and he designed and built a wooden winder that saved the boys from rolling all that string back up after the flight.

Together, the brothers stood on the packed earth on the crest of the tall, narrow hill, holding a kite, the winder, and several rolls of kite string. They aimed their kite straight up, avoiding the power lines and the trees that lined the Ohio River. If the wind was just right, it caught the sail, propelling the kite south over Huntington's rooftops or north over the creeping coal barges. The boy with the kite let the string zip off the roll, the handles spinning against his palms. Each time a roll ended, the brothers tied on a fresh one, keeping careful track of the number and length of the rolls. When they tired of flying, they cranked the mass of string onto the winder and penciled into a notebook how many feet the kite had soared.

Their best kite ever was a white paper Texaco model. In the center, a scarlet star framed a black capital T. The kite lasted for years; when it tore, snagged on a tree branch or their beagle's teeth, the boys patched the hole with glue and white paper.

They also had a Green Giant kite, a craft David earned by saving up green bean labels. He doesn't remember flying it, watching the vivid green man with his leafy tunic sailing over the more demure greens of the grass, oaks, and maples; he figures he must have lost it on the first flight. What my dad remembers is the kite's arrival. He was catching insects in his tiny front yard, and the mailman put the cellophane-wrapped kite directly in his hands. "Go fly a kite!" the mailman barked, almost rudely, but David chuckled. *Mary Poppins* was in the theater, and though his parents wouldn't let him visit that sinful place to see the film himself, he'd heard the other kids singing on the playground. "Let's go fly a kite!" He ran into the house, humming to himself, burning to fly his new kite with his brothers.

Then Mike got married and moved to Virginia, and David stayed in Huntington, married Marcy, and had the four of us kids. Mark lived with his parents until he was thirty. When I was tiny, a bedroom in my grandparents' relentlessly tidy house was cluttered with sweaty socks, fishing magazines, and the mesh running shorts Mark wore for his daily jogs. I liked to sneak under Mark's bed and touch the cool metal of his hunting rifles.

I trembled a little on those visits to my grandparents' house, waiting for my uncle's trim blond beard and hazel eyes to spring around a corner. I ran, but he always caught me. He held me upside down over the toilet, yelling, "You're going to get swallowed by Mr. Mess!" I clutched his sweatpants and screamed, the ends of my hair dripping toilet water.

When I was seven, Mark took a computer programming job in another West Virginia town, but he visited on the weekends, coming along when we birdwatched or canoed across Beech Fork Lake. For Christmas and birthdays, he bought flying objects for my siblings and me—kites, model rockets, remote-controlled airplanes—and he came with us to the park to try them out. We were the closest thing Mark had to children, and we enjoyed the gifts and extra attention, not realizing our uncle must have felt lonely sometimes when we were far away. On Christmas afternoons, my siblings and I put on our new mittens and piled into Mark's sporty white car. For hours, we squealed and shivered in a field, crashing an airplane into the muddy snow.

We saved the kites Mark bought us for the warm, windy spring, flying them at the base of a dam that resembled the grassy floodwall. The kite I remember best: a plastic portrait of Elmo. The red Muppet shone against a cerulean background. When Mark came with us, he flew the kite first, clearing the steep hill, avoiding a copse of trees. Finally, my turn came. I gripped the plastic handles on either side of the roll, watching, exultant, as Elmo sailed over the creek.

+ + +

MARK kept moving, further each time, until he came home only twice a year. On Christmas mornings, he videotaped our paper-tearing frenzy. On the Fourth of July, he washed his hotdogs down with Coke, then he jumped into my grandparents' aboveground pool with his brothers and zipped around until half the water splashed out. I know Mark canoed down the Potomac River with Mike a few times, but most of the year he must have been alone.

One autumn weekend, when Mark lived in East Bank, West Virginia, my dad and I visited him and went lake fishing at Babcock State Park. During the day, we cast from rocks on the lakeshore, our red-and-white bobbers floating among the fallen leaves. At night, we played computer games, then we lounged on sleeping bags beside Mark's orange chair and watched *Flintstones* cartoons. If he had any alcohol, he hid it well. Maybe he hadn't started drinking yet. That was years before he moved to Pennsylvania. We never found time to visit him again.

+ + +

THE last three years, we knew Mark was sick, but we didn't know what he had. He occasionally mentioned his treatments—blood transfusions, the fluid doctors drained from his stomach every few months, then every month, then every week—so we researched online and made guesses. Esophageal cancer? Acid reflux had plagued him for years.

Grandpa guessed Mark's liver might be involved, and he offered his son part of his own liver. Mark's voice was higher than his father's, but Grandpa deepened his voice to imitate Mark's stubborn refusal: "I don't want no liver transplant." I know Grandpa didn't believe then Mark was losing his liver to alcoholism. Months later, when he found Mark's liquor in his apartment before he died, Grandpa had just stepped in the sticky red-brown layer on his son's bathroom floor. Grandpa shook his head and muttered, "That pain was so bad, Mark bought him some whisky."

For a while, the software helpline Mark worked for let him answer calls from home. He thought about moving back to West Virginia, but he didn't. We would have found out he was drinking. Then his boss let him go, helping him apply for permanent disability checks. I heard her voice chirping on Mark's answering machine: "We'll all feel better when we've got you set up."

Bored and lonely, probably terrified, Mark called his parents and brothers more in six months than he had in the twenty years since he'd moved away. He seemed to lose track of the hour and the decade, berating my dad at two a.m. for wrongs committed on the floodwall. Mark was probably drunk, but my dad didn't realize this. "I'm so sorry," my dad told his brother, his voice groggy. He rarely remembered what Mark was talking about. If my dad asked Mark about his illness or offered to drive up and help, Mark slammed the receiver down and didn't call again for days.

Two months before Mark died, Rebecca drove up to visit him in the hospital on her college spring break. She worried he'd be angry, but they laughed for two hours, storytelling about fishing trips and my grandparents' pool, halving the dry slice of carrot cake that came with his bland roast beef and peas. His IV knocked loose, spattering his gown with blood, but he wouldn't let the nurse clean him up. "Sarah Beth, sit down! You're not leaving," he ordered. Rebecca cried all the way home.

A few weeks later, my dad and I tried to visit, but this time Mark was at his apartment. I made the mistake of e-mailing and asking permission. "Please don't come," he responded. "I'm really just trying to recover." We began to fear he'd die alone in his apartment. But Mark's doctor called in time.

The last day Mark could talk, he told me, "I love you, Rebecca." I didn't mind being Rebecca. Later, I thanked him for the carrot cake, pretending it was me who'd come to see him.

+ + +

I don't know where Mark flew his kite, but I imagine him in a park where I know he often walked. As he strode past a pond of ducks and belching bullfrogs, a playground of yelling children, a folksinger on a park bench with a guitar, Mark held out his cell phone so I could hear. "I'm going to the dollar store next. Do you need anything?" he asked me. It was almost like I was there.

One day, Mark asked Jennifer if she wanted a moon cactus. He was about to buy one for himself, and he could buy her one, too. "Yes," my sister answered, laughing. Surely he wasn't serious. The cactus came in the mail a few days later: a poppy-red knob on a prickly green stem. I imagine Mark whistling as he strolled back past the playground, the cactuses swinging in a bag at his side.

I like to think Mark got the idea to fly a kite on one of those evening walks. Passing an open field next to the bullfrog pond, he remembered flying that Texaco kite with his brothers. He walked faster, with new purpose. Later, at Walmart, he chose a high-performance nylon kite, designed for speed and tricks. A single adult with a good job, he could afford a nice kite. When he got home, no one would ask him why he blew money on a toy and forgot the milk. As he drove back to his apartment, he ignored the turnoff for the liquor store, remembering how Mike had gripped the kite string in his unlined hands, knocking another kite from the sky with a swift jerk.

"Mark was flying kites all the time for a while there," MaMa said after we opened Mark's trunk. "Then an old man looked at him funny and he never flew a kite again."

An old man. I wonder about that old man, a person whose glance destroyed one of my shy, lonely uncle's only joys in life. Looking at Mark, the man may have been thinking what a perfect day it was for a kite, or that he wished his grandchildren lived closer so he could teach them to fly. Mark must have read in the man's eyes the judgment he dreaded: kites ought to be flown by children, or with children, or at the very least with a giggling date. Solitary, bearded men with kites might be dangerous.

Mark stared at the grass as he wound up his kite string, yanking his kite from the sky. He slung the little aircraft into his trunk and banged the lid.

+ + +

I'VE forgotten the last time I flew a kite, but I remember the last time I wanted to fly one. I was in my early teens, and it was the first warm, windy Saturday of spring. Kite in the trunk of my dad's old work car, two little sisters in the backseat, I sat shotgun next to my dad as we joggled along the road to the dam. We were jubilant, singing songs about our beagle we made up as we went, imagining Elmo soaring higher and longer than ever. Then the car's peeling gray hood crumpled like tinfoil, shivering the windshield. My dad cursed as he slammed on the brakes, drumming the steering wheel with his fist. He must have left the hood unlatched after he checked the oil.

As we crept back home, my dad poked his head out the window like a carsick spaniel, watching the road. He worried loudly about how he'd get to work until he replaced that windshield. I mourned the kite, limp in the trunk. Something in me realized we wouldn't find time for it again.

The last time David flew a kite as a child, he was thirteen. His family had moved to the other side of Huntington, far away from the floodwall. His brother Mike had gone off to college, stashing his kite string machine in a box in the attic.

Determined to keep flying, David purchased a box kite, an angular flyer built for high elevation, and he set out alone in his new backyard on a blustery day. I imagine Mark's blond head at a window. David ran across the top of the hill behind his house and released his kite, unrolling the string slowly, watching the box soar for a moment above the neighbor's horses. Then a stiff wind snapped the string and carried the kite into the sky. Skinny shoulders bent, David trudged back toward the house clutching his roll, the frayed end dangling.

+ + +

WHEN I walked into Mark's apartment, I looked for alcohol. Until that trip to Pennsylvania, I'd assumed thoughtlessly that Mark was like my dad—that he'd never taken a drink in his life—but I knew the usual cause for Mark's diagnosis. At first, I saw only an empty case of Bud Light, and I tried to dismiss my suspicions. Perhaps Mark had simply been more normal than his teetotaling Baptist parents. A guy who enjoyed a beer during a Dallas Cowboys game.

I took another step and it surrounded me. Liquor bottles around the orange chair. Beer cases in the pantry. Liquor bottles in his dresser drawers, as if he'd hidden them when someone knocked. A sixteen-ounce glass of whisky on the living room floor: he had to have known that much could kill him. For a moment, I hoped Grandpa was right—that Mark had drunk when his painkillers failed him—then I found a five-year-old list of alcohol support centers, one number circled in blue. I wonder if he called.

Seeing Mark's alcohol hurt as badly as watching his final vial of medication run empty, as watching my dad collapse in the hospital elevator, sobbing. As listening for the rattle in Mark's lungs that meant it wasn't over. Mark had been so unhappy, and he hadn't told us. Of course, he couldn't tell his family about his drinking; we would have jumped in our cars and tried to stop him. But I worry that my uncle also dreaded our righteous judgment. Maybe he was afraid we'd think he deserved his dead liver. I hope *he* didn't think he deserved it. I have a glass of wine with a friend on occasion, but I don't talk about it at home. In my family, even one drink bears the taint of sin.

When I realized Mark was an alcoholic, I feared I'd never known him at all, and my dad felt the same way. Mark had been miserable, killing himself for years, and we had all failed to help him. Guilt overwhelmed me like nausea.

Before I left Mark's apartment, I found his moon cactus on a sunny windowsill. Cobwebs coated the head and stem, both parts shriveled and gray.

+ + +

ON my mission trip to Haiti at sixteen, I watched kites from a rooftop in the missionary compound during evening prayers.

Compared with my flashy red-and-blue Elmo kite, Haitian kites looked pitiful, constructed from willowy tree branches and beige plastic bags. But as the sun set, the bags glowed: orange, gold, violet, rose.

On that trip, I saw eight-year-olds perched on mountain-sides, hoeing the dirt between their bare feet. When the kites flooded the horizon in the evenings, those makeshift toys reminded me the tiny laborers were in fact children, and they knew as well as Americans how to play. Their day's work behind them, they could throw a kite in the air and escape, soaring above their crops on the mountainsides, the outhouses they shared with their villages.

Kite flying as an adult, perhaps Mark could have understood those children as he unrolled his kite string at the park. His kite glided above the silence that lurked behind his apartment door, the empty bedsheets he'd face again that night. Looking around, he saw couples with children, the white car that would carry him back to his apartment, alone. Looking up, he saw pink nylon and sky.